Rule of Fear

Rule of Fear

Human rights in South Africa

Catholic Institute for International Relations
British Council of Churches

First published 1989
Catholic Institute for International Relations, 22 Coleman Fields, London N1 7AF, UK, in association with British Council of Churches, Inter-Church House, 35-41 Lower Marsh, London SE1 7RL, UK
© CIIR 1989

British Library Cataloguing in Publication Data:
Rule of Fear: human rights in South Africa
  1. South Africa. Human rights. Deprivation
  I. Catholic Institute for International Relations
  323.4'9'0968

  ISBN 1 85287 056 7

Originally published in South Africa in May 1989 by the Human Rights Commission, the South African Council of Churches and the Southern African Catholic Bishops' Conference under the title *Human Rights and Repression in South Africa — the Apartheid Machine Grinds On.* Many chapters first presented as papers at the Bonn *Human Rights in South Africa* conference organised in June 1989 by the Association of West European Parliamentarians for Action against Apartheid.

Cover and text design by Keith Addison
Cover photo: Afrapix
Printed in the UK by Russell Press Ltd, Nottingham

Contents

Preface .... *vii*

Foreword *1*

1. The legal system *5*

2. Repression under security legislation *9*

3. Repression under the State of Emergency *15*

4. Informal repression *20*

5. 'Winning hearts and minds' *28*

6. Censorship *33*

7. Human rights in the homelands *36*

8. Land and homelessness *45*

9. Repression and trade unions *52*

10. Education for inequality *61*

11. Militarisation and white South Africa *68*

12. Human rights and conscientious objection *73*

13. Destabilisation in Southern Africa *79*

14. The cost of apartheid *83*

15. Conclusion *91*

Postscript *95*

Abbreviations *97*

Preface

A fierce debate has sprung up in the British media about the right of individual cricketers to take up lucrative contracts in South Africa. The controversy hinges on the denial of human rights to the majority of that country's people.

In South Africa, violations of human rights are not merely occasional or matters of inconvenience. As this book clearly sets out, the violations are related to the law of the land, the whole body of which has for generations systematically denied every basic human right recognised by international convention. The fundamental injustice of apartheid, now reinforced by four years of emergency 'rule by decree', violates the rights of millions of black South Africans to life, food, shelter, land, education, freedom of expression, movement and employment, freedom to organise politically and in the workplace and, crucially, the right to vote for their country's government.

As President Botha bows out and a new face takes over, supported by a continuing though much reduced majority in the all white Parliament, the West is again being wooed with suggestions that reform will go ahead if international pressure can be dropped. Meanwhile, political opponents languish in prison or under house arrest and hundreds are judicially executed in what has become the hanging capital of the world. Others, even young children, are detained and tortured and even more fall victim to unnamed vigilantes or hit squads. The organisations that voice the aspirations of the majority are banned and media restrictions mean that news is either blocked by a wall of silence or distorted by selective releases.

We in Britain have a special responsibility to hear the voices of the oppressed in South Africa and to take action in support of their cause. We have long-standing historical, cultural, religious and economic links with the ruling minority. Our government has steadfastly opposed the call from the South African churches and unions for sanctions sufficient to end apartheid.

For the churches in particular, it is vital to show solidarity with fellow Christians like those who, on 1 September 1989, stood peacefully outside security police headquarters in the centre of Cape Town and were lashed, beaten and arrested. They were wearing T-shirts with a message that calls Christians everywhere to stand beside them: 'Standing for the Truth: Christians defy unjust laws'.

Philip Morgan
General Secretary, British Council of Churches

Ian Linden
General Secretary, Catholic Institute for International Relations

September 1989

Foreword

A partheid is a social system which not only violates virtually every one of the 30 articles of the Universal Declaration of Human Rights, but is fundamentally opposed to it. Unlike in any other country, the abuse of human rights in South Africa is institutionalized in its constitution, its statute books, its parliament, its political practice and the consciousness of the ruling minority. Violations have been perpetrated in pursuit of conquest and domination in a system where the ends justify the means, regardless of the injury to the human spirit. The four pillars of apartheid, the Group Areas Act, the Population Registration Act, the Separate Amenities Act and the Land Act are reinforced by the plethora of racist laws which dispossess our people of their land and wealth. The Emergency regulations, refined over the 34-month-long National State of Emergency, have intensified repression.

The law courts consistently interpret the law and the Emergency regulations in favour of the state rather than the individual, particularly in the case of blacks. This comes as no surprise since the legislature represents the white minority, whilst the courts are turned into organs of the apartheid system to punish those who resist it.

Our security legislation, developed over 25 years, upholds indefinite detention without trial. Since the beginning of the State of Emergency, over 50,000 have been detained, 15,000 of whom were children under the age of 18. These prisoners of conscience are incarcerated without legal recourse in apartheid's jails which history will brand as the concentration camps of South Africa. Sixty-seven people have died in detention.

Our young people's generation will carry the scars of solitary confinement, torture and extreme deprivation.

Another weapon in the arsenal of repression is the restriction order which, once gazetted, provides no legal avenue for appeal. Scores of individuals, and, most recently, activists released from detention, have

1

been silenced and, in many cases, house arrested and effectively denied the right to work. A restriction order simply exchanges one jail for another: ex-detainees are condemned to a half-life outside, shackled by laws which restrict their lives as effectively as prison walls and regulations. Since 1945, 50 democratic organisations have been banned. In 1988, 33 organisations, including the UDF, COSATU and AZAPO, have fallen under the axe of the restriction order.

Pretoria's gallows, dubbed 'South Africa's death-factory', have executed over 1,070 people in the last decade, a frightening statistic which positions South Africa as the world leader in hangings. The majority of those on death-row are victims of apartheid, whose crimes are rooted in their impoverished and socially deprived backgrounds. Of approximately 290, 80 have been sentenced for political acts. Executions have become yet another means of silencing political opponents.

Forced removals continue unabated. Millions have lost their homes, land and means of survival. Like pawns they are moved around to populate the regime's bantustans and to perpetuate the segregation of residential areas. The newly promulgated Prevention of Illegal Squatting Act will ensure that millions more will be left homeless. The humiliation and cruelty gains momentum.

The system of compulsory military conscription gives the young white South African man no choice. Either he must take up arms against his compatriots in defence of apartheid, or he must follow his conscience and go to jail or become an involuntary exile.

In the face of these aberrations, the state vainly attempts to maintain a veneer of stability and a pretence of normality by controlling information by decree. Courageous newspapers have been attacked, suspended and banned, many journalists restricted and silenced for exercising their fundamental freedom of expression and exposing the truth.

Even the church has become a target of the regime, as those ministers and Christians who feel bound to 'stand for the truth' in our land and bear a prophetic witness against apartheid become victims of state and right-wing propaganda, detentions, and sinister and violent attacks.

This catalogue of human rights abuses is by no means exhaustive, but it does demonstrate the evil and sickness of the social order which we are committed to ending. The history of our struggle for political rights is the chronicle of a proud and courageous fight for human rights and justice. Over the years, a human rights culture has evolved in the

Working for a new South Africa: A peace ribbon displayed in Johannesburg, with the words 'A place in the sun for everyone.'

Anna Ziemir·ski, Afrapix

struggle for change. The decades of opposition to exploitation and oppression culminated in the massive popular resistance of the 1980s. The devastating repression of the State of Emergency ushered in state reform on the backs of Casspirs – reform which is meaningless and without legitimacy, which our people will continue to reject until apartheid is dismantled.

The regime may have maimed a generation and banned its organisations, but it has fatally underestimated the spirit of resistance enshrined in the consciousness of the people. The recent hunger strike, a humbling lesson for us all, bears witness to this. It re-focused world attention on the plight of detainees and the abhorrent laws which, with the flick of a bureaucrat's pen, condemned tens of thousands to a sub-human existence. Their courageous 'life and death' struggle elicited an unprecedented response from the state: it was not a township revolt that they could easily quell by sending in their Casspirs. The act of the detainees rendered the sophisticated and brutal killing machine of apartheid powerless, forcing the government to negotiate meaningfully. Through their sacrificial act the hunger strikers created the climate conducive to meaningful negotiation. This will remain as one of the most powerful and inspiring examples of the pressure that can be generated by those who seem to be least free and most powerless.

A demand for human rights is a demand for freedom, and for justice, for political change, and most importantly, a non-negotiable demand for the abolition of apartheid to make way for a new order. It will be a new order in which all South Africans, blacks and whites, will live together in a non-racial democratic society where the rights of the individual will be sacred and inviolate.

Frank Chikane
General Secretary – South African Council of Churches

1. The legal system

The franchise and race

The government is frequently at pains to eulogise the South African legal system. There is indeed much that is commendable in the Roman-Dutch and English foundations of South African law. However, fundamental rights and freedoms have been systematically eroded by radical legislative intervention. The doctrine of parliamentary sovereignty decrees that Parliament may pass any law it chooses, no matter how unnecessary, arbitrary or evil, and it is the function of the courts to give effect to Parliament's will. In a democracy, this doctrine is unobjectionable. If the electorate is dissatisfied with its rulers it may elect new ones in a general election. In South Africa, however, access to the ballot box is deliberately denied to the majority of citizens.

The most fundamental civil right, the right to vote, is confined to those who are classified as 'white'. In 1984, those classified as 'coloured' and 'Indian' were extended a token vote with power effectively remaining in the hands of the white minority. Those classified 'black' are totally excluded. Racial classification which is defined in terms of artificial criteria such as 'general appearance' and 'general acceptance' is the key to political power and regulates virtually every facet of life. The right to own and occupy property, to educate one's children and to have access to health care, are all dictated by skin colour.

Basic apartheid laws

Some of the main legislated pillars of apartheid are:
* *The Population Registration Act of 1950.* This act presumes to identify and classify from birth each person as belonging to one of

---

LEGAL CHARADE

'However neatly one may attempt to organise or, rather, dress up the proceedings in courtrooms, it is nothing other than an attempt... to camouflage what really is at stake – apartheid.'

– International Jurist

'One thing emerges from our contacts... for most of these people there is no distinction between the departments involved in the legal process – the courts are perceived as an extension of the police and prison systems.'

– Black Sash report

---

four distinct races, and determines the destiny of each individual in terms of franchise, mobility, residential rights and social benefits and services provided by the state. This is the basic apartheid act. If it was repealed, all other apartheid acts would become inoperable, including the constitution.

- *The Reservation of Separate Amenities Act of 1953.* According to this act, each individual, classified under the Population Registration Act, is meted out educational and other social subsidies and has access to certain facilities, which differ greatly according to race.
- *The Development Trust and Land Act of 1936 and the Native Land Act of 1913.* This legislation allocated 13.6% of the land to 70% of the population in South Africa. Blacks may not buy or own land outside these areas allocated for blacks (which form the homelands).
- *The Group Areas Act of 1966* (first promulgated 1950). This seeks to effect a total social and residential separation between the four identified race groups (and makes a mockery of the hailed scrapping of the Prohibition of Mixed Marriages Act).
- *The Prevention of Illegal Squatting Act of 1989* (first promulgated 1951). Greater penalties than ever before exist for squatters and the homeless as well as anyone who permits 'squatting' on their premises, while the power of the courts to intervene and prevent removals of squatters has been severely eroded.

The last three laws, coupled with the Homeland Citizenship Act of 1970, and a chronic shortage of housing in the allocated black areas, are the new form of influx control in South Africa. The latter act is the instrument whereby black people are forced by residence in designated 'independent' homeland areas, to be citizens of that homeland,

and denied South African nationality, the right to work freely in South Africa, obtain passports and travel documents for international travel, etc.

- *The Bantu Homelands Constitution Act of 1971* (later called the Black States Constitution Act), is the act which allowed for the creation of such homelands. The territories allocated are by size and lack of resources unable to be self-sufficient, and the survival of these areas is dependent on the continuing financial support of South Africa. Of course, such support means significant, if not decisive, control.

Resistance and repression

The denial of political power to the black majority inevitably spawned resistance, initially passive in nature and eventually taking the form of armed revolt. Drastic security measures, initially intended to be of temporary duration only, soon became permanent features of the law designed to stem the rising tide of opposition. Detention without trial for the purposes of interrogation, the power to restrict individuals and organisations, and powers of censorship all form part of the ordinary laws of the land. These laws are supplemented by special powers promulgated under the various states of emergency. The political system is characterised by the denial of those basic rights which are inherent in any democracy.

The judiciary

It is against this background that the role of the judiciary, frequently proclaimed by the government to be among the finest in the world, must be assessed. The absence of a Bill of Rights necessarily limits the powers of the judiciary in an unjust legal order. Although the powers of the courts are limited, judges are by no means impotent. On the contrary, they are able to protect individuals from the abuse of power in a number of ways. For example, where legislation is ambiguous, a judge is entitled to adopt an interpretation which avoids harshness and injustice. The Supreme Court is also empowered to ensure that those entrusted with discretionary powers exercise them fairly, for proper purposes and without ulterior motive.

The classic function of the courts is to administer justice to those who seek it without fear, favour or prejudice, independently of the

---

RELATIVE FREEDOM

'The court is free as it were as a fish is free, to swim in a net.'

– President Paul Kruger

---

consequences which ensue. The ability of the judiciary to fulfil this function has often been obstructed and even removed altogether by legislation which has stripped the courts of their traditional powers. In addition, the willingness of the courts to protect individuals from executive excess has been dubious. The all-white Supreme Court bench is not perceived to be a champion of justice. In 1968, the International Commission of Jurists (ICJ) observed that 'in spite of a number of courageous decisions at first instance, the overall impression is of a judiciary as "establishment-minded" as the executive, prepared to adopt an interpretation that will facilitate the executive's task rather than defend the liberty of the subject and uphold the Rule of Law'. Twenty years later, the ICJ was to comment that 'if a judge remains on the bench in such a repressive regime, there can be no excuse for failing to exercise his choice in favour of individual liberty, and whereas some judges have done justice in such cases in recent times, the majority of the South African bench have failed to do so'.

Ultimately, any system which institutionalises racial discrimination and which uses the law to perpetrate political, social and economic inequality is incompatible with justice. It is this system itself which has brought the entire administration of justice into disrepute.

The UN Declaration of Human Rights

Article 11: Everyone charged with a penal offence has the right to be presumed innocent until proven guilty according to law in a public trial at which he has all the guarantees necessary for his defence.

---

2. Repression under security legislation

I n 1982 the government introduced the Internal Security Act (ISA) No 74 to streamline and consolidate previous security legislation. This act superseded but included major aspects of the old ISA of 1976, the Terrorism Act of 1967 and the General Laws Amendment Act of 1963. This legislation has served as the basis and justification of many acts of repression in South Africa.

Severe inroads have been made into the freedom of individuals – their speech, their association, their right to a fair trial. This, of course, has been supported and consolidated by the State of Emergency. It has provided the security forces with a vast range of powers in the enactment of repression against forces working for change within the country. The issues below provide some insight into the level of repression in this country and the extent to which democracy has been eroded.

Detention without trial

Security legislation has allowed for the detention of people without trial for the purposes of interrogation. Police have been granted arbitrary powers through security legislation which culminated in the 1982 Internal Security Act.

The ISA of 1982 contained four sections that provided for the detention of people deemed by the security police as being a danger to state security.

Section 29 is the most notorious of these provisions. It empowers a security officer to hold a person indefinitely, specifically for the purposes of interrogation. Detainees are kept in solitary confinement.

9

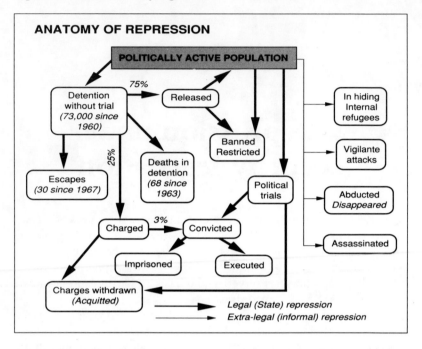

ANATOMY OF REPRESSION

It is from these detainees that many allegations of torture and abuse have stemmed.

Section 28 allowed for indefinite preventive detention. It is used to remove activists from circulation in order to cripple the organisations to which they belong or to block them from an initiative in which they may be participating. This section does not allow for interrogation.

Section 31 allows an officer of the court rather than a security officer to detain a person who can act as a potential state witness. The period of detention may not exceed six months, or the duration of the trial in which their evidence is required. However, given the duration of some political trials, it is not uncommon for detainees to be held for up to two years.

Section 50 introduced a 14-day period of preventive detention. A low-ranking police officer may detain a person deemed to be threatening public safety. For further detention after 14 days, permission must be granted by a magistrate. Usually, people held under this clause are transferred to section 29 detention before the 14 days expire. Others are released before that date.

Strict division: An SADF patrol erects a fence around KTC squatter camp in Cape Town after raids by vigilantes.

Adil Bradlow, Afrapix

In addition to the above, the four 'independent' homelands have evolved their own respective security legislation modelled on the legislation of South Africa. From 1963 to the first six months of 1988, 21,863 detentions under security legislation had taken place.

Detentions under security legislation

	Interrogation	Witness	Preventive	Homelands	Total
1987	532	84	–	286	902
1988 (6 months)	149	1	–	28	178

Legislation also exists in the form of the Protection of Information Act of 1984 which prevents the press from publicising certain detentions.

Banning of persons under the ISA

Persons may be banned under the ISA which usually includes confinement to a particular district, prohibition from attending any kind of gathering and prevention from being quoted. In some cases,

11

house arrest is included in the banning order which results in the person being confined to his or her house for a specified period each day. On 10 February 1986 ten people were banned under sections 19(1) and 20 of the ISA. No persons have been banned under security legislation since 1986; the State of Emergency legislation has been used for this purpose.

Bannings of meetings under the ISA

Since 1976 all outdoor political meetings have been banned unless held with the permission of a magistrate or the minister of law and order. Ministerial bans were also imposed on indoor political meetings. All meetings concerning school or student boycotts and work stoppages or stayaways are also banned. However, in April 1987 the minister of law and order relaxed the restrictions on funerals and genuine sports meetings.

The minister of law and order, Mr Adriaan Vlok, said in Parliament that 316 people were arrested for attending prohibited gatherings under the ISA during 1987 (Hansard (a) 5 q col 352, 8 March).

Bannings of organisations under the ISA

Bannings of organisations have taken place under security legislation since the 1960s. Up to 1966, five organisations were banned under the Suppression of Communism Act. Thereafter 19 organisations have been banned under the Internal Security Act. The similar security legislation in the 'independent' homelands has resulted in the bannings of 42 organisations.

Listings

In terms of section 56(1) of the ISA no 'utterance, speech and statement' of a listed person may be published or disseminated without the permission of the minister of law and order. The penalty for quoting such a person is a prison sentence of up to three years or a fine. In August 1988 a new consolidated list of people whom it was illegal to quote was gazetted. Of the 417 names, 117 were living abroad in exile, 20 were deceased and the remaining 280 were either resident in South Africa or serving sentences in South African prisons.

Political trials

The courts have operated as an arena where those deemed to be a threat to public safety have been charged and convicted. There has been an enormous escalation of the number of political trials in recent years. In the year ending June 1988, for example, 51 political trials involving 165 people were completed with 80 convictions and 85 acquittals. A further 58 trials were in progress, involving 258 accused. (This figure included 195 people who were on trial for treason following a coup d'etat in Bophuthatswana.) The charges ranged from treason, terrorism, membership of banned organisations, sabotage, military training, harbouring and illegal gathering to such offences as murder and public violence, which at first glance are not political, yet upon close investigation prove to be so. Many are also charged under the Internal Security Act. According to the minister of law and order, a total of 81 people were charged with offences under the Internal Security Act during 1987. Two were acquitted, two were convicted of lesser offences and 71 were still on trial or awaiting trial as at February 1988.

A prominent trend among these trials was to prosecute important community leaders on tenuous charges involving allegations of conspiracy with the ANC and plotting to overthrow the state by making townships ungovernable. The thinness of the evidence has not saved them from conviction and harsh sentencing by judges. The best known of these cases is the 'Delmas Trial' which tied up three senior leaders of the UDF and various religious and civic leaders in a trial which took three years to end. It is significant that only five of the original 22 accused were actually jailed, receiving lengthy sentences.

UN Declaration of Human Rights

Article 9: No-one shall be subjected to arbitrary arrest, detention or exile.

TORTURE – FACTS AND FIGURES

- In a study of detainees between 1974 and 1984, 38.5% said they had had no access to external light; 42.7% had received no clean clothing; 38.4% had no exercise opportunity; 50% had no access to reading material; 58.4% received no food parcels; 22.9% had no contact with anyone except the authorities. In the sample used in the study, 132 out of 176 (or 75%) were detained for longer than two months (60 days) and some for up to almost two years.

- In the study, 83% of the ex-detainees said they had been physically tortured. Torture included beating, forced standing, maintaining abnormal body positions, forced gymnasium-type exercises, electric shock, strangulation, suspension, chains, genital abuse, pulling out or burning hair, beating or burning soles of the feet, being thrown in the air and allowed to fall, given salted water to drink, being set alight, breasts squeezed, held out of a moving car, placed in boot of car, hands cut with a knife, fingernails burnt or crushed with a brick, being tied to a tree, being scrubbed on face and body with a hard brush.

- In the study, all the ex-detainees reported some form of psychological torture including false accusations, solitary confinement, verbal abuse, threats of violence, contradictory styles of interrogation, being given misleading information, threats of violence to family, forced to undress, constant interrogation, being blindfolded, sleep deprivation, threats of prolonged detention, sham executions, drug administration, excrement abuse, use of animals.

- In 1987 a panel of doctors who treat freed detainees in Johannesburg released a study alleging that 72% of those seen claimed they were assaulted in detention, and of these 97% showed signs of abuse. The South African Police said it was 'a pity' they were expected to reply to serious allegations about the treatment of detainees 'which are not substantiated in any manner whatever'.

Said a police spokesperson:

'What seems to be conveniently overlooked is the strict code of discipline which ensures that all detainees are properly cared for, that they are not assaulted and that they receive proper medical, spiritual and other care.'

The doctors said detainees had evidence of bruises, lacerations, perforated eardrums and gunshot wounds.

(Sources: 'Detention and Torture in South Africa' by Don Foster; The Star, 8 April 1987; New Nation, 9 April 1987)

3. Repression under the State of Emergency

The declaration of the State of Emergency

Mass resistance and protest against the apartheid policies of the South African government exploded in August/September 1984 in the face of attempts by the government to formalise the exclusion of the black majority from political power through the introduction of the Tri-Cameral Parliament and unrepresentative Black Local Councils. Unacceptable rent increases triggered further anger and frustration, which were met by an invasion of the townships by the army. On 21 July 1985 a partial State of Emergency was declared in 32 magisterial districts. This was lifted seven months later only to be reimposed, throughout the country, on 12 June 1986. Since then the Total State of Emergency has been redeclared annually in June and is currently in its fourth year.

The reason given for the declaration of the Emergency was that a 'revolutionary climate' existed which it was not possible to control using the ordinary laws of the land. The ordinary laws of the land are in fact extraordinary, so why were emergency powers needed? Three main reasons are:

- Powers of arrest and detention without warrant are given to the lowest ranking policemen and soldiers (10,000 people were detained in the first three weeks of the total emergency);
- Security forces are granted virtual indemnity for their actions;
- Strict media control can be enforced, thereby ensuring a blackout on information, as in wartime.

Take it away: A policeman removes a Black Sash poster, despite protests from one of the organisation's members.

Paul Weinberg, Afrapix

Powers under the State of Emergency

The powers assumed by the authorities under the State of Emergency are very considerable, and although many were challenged in court in the early stages, they have now become virtually impregnable through modification and several Appeal Court judgements.

These powers include:

Control over persons, through indefinite detention without trial (including interrogation), restriction orders on released detainees or other persons and regulation of movement in and out of specified areas;

- Control over gatherings, through banning meetings, limiting attendance and actions at funerals, and enforcing 'legalised' powers to
break up gatherings;
- Control over organisations, through restriction orders forbidding
certain listed activities or any activity whatsoever by specified
organisations;
- Control over the media, by placing an embargo on reporting any
security force action, and reporting (or even being present at) any
'unrest' incident, apart from supplying the police version of such
happenings. In addition there are numerous other restrictions,
combined with the power to suspend or close down offending
publications;
- Banning of any boycott or stayaway forms of protest;
- Control over presence or movement in and out of schools and over
what may be taught and what clothing may be worn;
- Power of entry, search and seizure without warrant.

Effects of the State of Emergency

There has been a drastic impact upon all aspects of life stretching
across all sectors of the population, particularly the black community,
as a result of actions taken by the state under the Emergency powers.

Over 50,000 persons have suffered the experience of detention
without trial during the last four years, some of them for periods of
more than three years. For many of them their status can be likened to
prisoners-of-war, interned pending the cessation of hostilities. The
major target has been the leadership and rank-and-file supporters of
the United Democratic Front (UDF) and its affiliates. To the everlasting
shame of the South African Government, more than one quarter of this
huge number have been children and young people, and over 10%
have been women.

Another drastic incursion into individual liberty is the now extensive
use of Restriction Orders, mainly served on released detainees whom
the minister of law and order was obliged to set free because they
embarked upon tenacious hunger strikes. Nearly 1,000 persons are
now restricted in terms of their freedom of movement, ability to engage
in political activity, earn a living or study.

Thirty-two anti-apartheid organisations, including the UDF, have
been banned from engaging in any activity whatsoever, while another,

---

DEATH OF A DETAINEE

A prison warder watched for 20 minutes while a young detainee wrapped a jersey around his neck, climbed onto a toilet below the cell's window, tied the arm of the garment to a bar on the window and slid from the toilet to his death.

Xoliso 'Dicky' Jacob's death occurred barely 24 hours before a certificate arrived, authorising his release after five months in Emergency detention, an Upington inquest court heard this week.

Warder Pienaar told Magistrate L.J. Brandt the 20-year-old detainee had spent most of his detention in solitary confinement. He had been on a spare diet for one month.

Pienaar said at about 9.30pm on 22 October 1986, he had seen Xoliso tie the sleeve of his blue jersey to the bar of his cell window. The young detainee had told him he would hang himself as soon as he had written to a police lieutenant asking why he had been detained when he had done nothing wrong.

The warder went to call a prison sergeant. When they and another warder arrived back at the cell, Xoliso had tied the jersey around his neck.

Pienaar said he watched Xoliso tie his jersey sleeve to the window, slowly slide off the toilet and hang from the garment. 'All the time he did not speak or make any noise,' the warder said.

When the other warders returned with a master key, 15 to 20 minutes later, they hauled Xoliso down, but he did not respond to heart massage.

Pienaar said the warders took the detainee outside the cell and placed him on a concrete slab. They did not summon doctors or nurses to the scene.

(From the Weekly Mail, 27 March 1987)

---

the Congress of South African Trade Unions (COSATU), the biggest trade union federation, is forbidden to engage in any 'political' activity.

Protest meetings and demonstrations are largely a thing of the past, and action of that kind is quickly countered by the state using banning orders and often brutal intervention.

Black township life is pervaded by the presence of the police and the army, and any attempts by township communities to organise their own residents' structures are closely monitored and subject to harassment.

Prime targets for the attention of the security forces are young people and students. Special restrictions apply to schools (see above) and the slightest attempt at political activity or organisation inevitably leads to detention. This is a particularly sensitive point of friction, since inferior black education is one of the foundation stones of the design of Grand Apartheid, and has long been a source of great anger.

The media operate under suffocating restrictions, with every editor working in tandem with a lawyer for fear of falling foul of the complex Emergency regulations. Several newspapers have suffered suspension for periods of up to three months, and others work under constant threat of closure. A curtain has fallen on much of what is happening in South Africa in a State of Emergency.

The uneasy equilibrium

In spite of the extreme, all-pervading repression of the Emergency, it is clear that resistance has not collapsed. Simple evidence of this is the fact that the authorities still find it necessary to continue with the State of Emergency, in order, in their own words, to maintain physical control over the 'continuing revolutionary situation'. Resistance has not disappeared. Rather, it has changed from an overt, publicly challenging form to a more guarded and even underground operation.

This presents the South African government with a major dilemma. It needs Emergency powers to contain resistance, yet it cannot afford to continue the State of Emergency for several reasons: foreign investor confidence has been shattered with the result that there has been a huge flight of capital, instead of the inflow that the country so desperately needs; the legitimacy of the government is seriously being questioned, both internationally and internally; concern is mounting in the white community over the morality of defending apartheid by force and over the growing isolation of South Africa

---

UN Declaration of Human Rights

Article 13: Everyone has the right to life, liberty and the security of person.

19

4. Informal repression

Under this heading, we identify a number of different activities which we describe as informal repression. These fall into two broad categories: (a) those activities carried out by organisations and structures which fall unambiguously under state control, and which operate with full legal sanction; and (b) activities which are clearly beyond the law, but which are pro-government or pro-apartheid, and which are carried out by anonymous agents or organisations, perhaps linked to the state, or by surrogate or right wing groups. What all these activities have in common, is that they frequently step beyond the bounds of the law, and their activities are very seldom successfully investigated or the culprits punished.

Legally sanctioned control and repression

In 1987, a major new development in the government's reform policies was the decentralisation of repressive power to regional and local levels, administered by Joint Management Councils (JMCs), reaching into townships, factories and rural communities. The JMCs implement the dual aspects of government policy: reform and repression. Reform takes the shape of providing services and infrastructure which are genuinely needed, and which may improve some aspects of people's lives. Repression, which is exerted simultaneously, removes from circulation the leaders of the communities who articulate grievances and political aspirations. These leaders are either detained, forced into hiding (hampering their ability to organise politically) or subjected to campaigns of intimidation. The JMC strategy appears to be to meet some of the community's expressed demands without giving credit to those who raised public awareness about it.

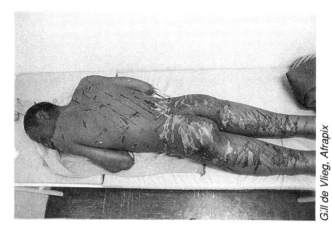

The cruelty of the vigilantes: A young victim from Thabong in the Orange Free State shows his wounds.

Gill de Vlieg, Afrapix

The new municipal police

The main vehicle for repressive control under the JMCs is the new police force created to serve the needs of the unpopular Black Local Authorities. It has been noted that these municipal police are poorly trained (mainly by means of crash courses of three to six months) and a good number of them have been identified as township thugs or former bodyguards of councillors. The 'kitskonstabels' (instant police), as they are known, have an appalling record of discipline, and are frequently accused of assault. In October 1987, the minister of law and order, in answer to a Parliamentary question, admitted that the guns issued to kitskonstabels had been used in at least 95 crimes, ranging from murder to rape and armed robbery. A survey in the Eastern Cape by the Black Sash revealed three major trends in municipal police activity: first, they were used to strengthen the power of community councillors; second, they act as auxiliaries to the South African Police, especially Security Police; third, they have close links with vigilantes, often siding with them in confrontations with democratic community organisations.

Extra-legal or surrogate repression

Another aspect of informal repression is ostensibly illegal, yet – even if not officially sanctioned – appears to enjoy a less than enthusiastic investigation. The activities detailed below are seldom brought to court, let alone successfully prosecuted. The activities are secretive and often more violent than other forms of repression. We refer here to attacks on individuals and property, such as the massive blast that destroyed Khotso House in Johannesburg, a building housing the South African Council of Churches (SACC) and anti-apartheid organisations (see page 24). In the same vein, 'vigilante' groups abound that attack progressive groups and their members. There is a disturbing tendency for these vigilantes to be recruited into the new municipal police units, and it is often difficult to recognise the difference between the two, save that the latter wear uniforms and the arms they carry are officially sanctioned.

In the past 18 months, a new trend has emerged. It marks a serious change in direction by police in terms of control of the townships. In 1985, 66% of people killed in township unrest were killed by the police. In 1987-88, the overwhelming majority of deaths are due to what government commentators refer to as 'black on black violence'. By stressing this, the impression is created that the state and its security forces are playing a peacekeeping role, and that the black community is tearing itself asunder.

The change in police tactics emerged after the enormous political opprobrium which descended on the police after the Langa massacre (21 March 1985) in which 22 died and over 50 were wounded (the state paid R1.3 million in compensation), and the Mamelodi massacre (21 November 1985), in which 12 people were killed. The change took a number of forms: first, the police became more pro-active, banning meetings, rallies and funerals rather than breaking them up while in progress; second, they controlled numbers who could attend, and laid down restrictions on the conduct of the occasions; third, they allowed free rein to vigilantes, who perform the same divisive and disruptive work which the police formerly undertook.

A graph of deaths in township violence in recent years would show that, as deaths due to police action declined, the total number of deaths did not decline accordingly; in fact, in some areas, such as Natal, it increased. The victims of the violence are largely the same – members of organisations belonging to the broad democratic movement and trade unionists, but the perpetrators of the killings had a new identity; they were black. However, the groups are generally identifiable in their support of broad aspects of apartheid policy. For example, the Ama Afrika group in Port Elizabeth, led by the Rev Ebenezer Maqina, has conducted a concerted campaign, sometimes amounting to war,

Informal repression: Residents of Crossroads squatter camp flee after an attack by Witdoek vigilantes in 1986.

Afrapix

against UDF and COSATU members. This is a form of 'surrogate' repression.

The most significant of such groups is the Inkatha organisation, based in Natal. It is tribalist in ideology, regards Natal as its fiefdom, and is intolerant of other organisations that are operating in its sphere of influence. Despite its mobilisation along ethnic (Zulu) lines, Inkatha has met with only mixed success. In particular, it is losing ground among youth, especially schoolchildren, the urbanised, and the workers. Over the last two years, Inkatha members have been involved in one of the most sustained periods of brutality ever witnessed in the Natal region. Here, the methods of confrontation and violence are blatant, in contrast to Inkatha's public image of moderation and negotiation.

Intimidation, violence and assassination

The year 1988 witnessed a steady tempo of kidnappings and assassinations of anti-apartheid activists. These took place both within South Africa's borders and in foreign countries.

Attacks on individuals and property

A large number of attacks on individuals and property have taken place recently. The main purpose seems to be intimidation. A low-intensity war is being waged in South Africa, with guerrillas of the ANC engaging in 'armed propaganda' in the form of bomb blasts in strategic places. These have brought retaliation from pro-apartheid forces in the form of massive demolition blasts at COSATU House (the Johannesburg-based head office of the largest trade union federation in South Africa), Community House in Cape Town (which housed a large number of progressive community organisations and trade unions), and Johannesburg's Khotso House (bombed in August 1988, which housed the South African Council of Churches, the Black Sash and many other church or anti-apartheid organisations).

These massive attacks on property can be crippling to organisations. Combined with the physical loss of irreplaceable records is the need to find new premises – a difficult task, as potential landlords are learning the intended lesson of the bomb blasts: it could be you next. The sophistication of the explosive devices, their size and expert placement all point to a military or para-military connection. However, there have also been bomb placements which appear to be by right-wing organisations aimed at the black population, such as a bomb placed in September 1988 in the Why Not Discotheque in Hillbrow, Johannesburg, a venue supported by a black clientele. These bombs have an intimidatory effect, and appear to be meant as a warning to black South Africans who are moving into areas previously reserved for whites only.

'Mysterious' robberies

The past 18 months have witnessed an escalation in robberies and break-ins at the offices and property of trade union and political organisations. This is particularly common in the Eastern Cape. Frequently, the only items stolen are important documents belonging to the organisations, leading the victims to suspect the Security Police. On other occasions, valuable equipment, including personal computers (which store important organisational information), typewriters, etc., have been stolen. These have caused considerable disruption of work. The same organisations have also been subjected to arson attacks that have destroyed premises and property.

Vigilante power:
The remains of a
settlement
outside Durban
after an attack.

Billy Paddock

Dirty tricks campaigns

Progressive organisations have been subject to numerous dirty tricks campaigns. The most common form of this activity is the production of pamphlets or publicity material purporting to be from a progressive organisation, but which carry a disruptive message. The purpose of the dirty tricks campaigns is to sow confusion and to promote internecine argument and fighting. In Soweto the two main (but rival) anti-apartheid groups, UDF and AZAPO, have been particularly singled out for this treatment. The perpetrators of the campaigns have never been brought to justice, but events relating to the End Conscription Campaign (ECC) are revealing. Here, three members of an army 'dirty tricks' unit had second thoughts and told the ECC of their activities. They were court-martialled, but a subsequent court action by ECC drew an admission by the army of their direct involvement. Thus we know that military intelligence was involved in at least this issue. There are two other intelligence agencies in South Africa: the Security Police and the National Intelligence System (NIS), both of which take a keen interest in progressive organisations and disruption.

Kidnappings and disappearances

Disappearance and/or kidnapping of activists continues. The kidnappings take two major forms: the abduction of activists from neighbouring countries and internal abductions. In the latter, some of the 'disappeared' people have subsequently been discovered in detention, but some disappear permanently.

One problem in solving these cases is the secrecy of the activities of the Security Police and the detention system. Disappeared activists may be detained, in hiding, in exile, or dead. This confusion works to the benefit of those who would disrupt political organisations, and is particularly welcomed by members of death squads. In one instance, Vusi Mashabane, from Duduza, was abducted, interrogated and tortured by a group of men who, it later transpired, were soldiers. Most alarming is the disappearance of Stanza Bopape, an important Pretoria activist from the Mamelodi Civic Association and employed by the Community Research and Information Centre (CRIC). The police say that he escaped from detention on 12 June 1988; however, he has never reappeared, and police led his family to believe he was still in detention for some time after this date.

Assassinations

Assassinations have the effect of controlling government opposition when all other methods, such as detention or intimidation, have failed. It is very rare indeed for perpetrators of assassinations to be brought to justice. An exception is the death of Eric Mntonga, an IDASA director in East London. Due to internal rivalries in the Ciskei Security Police, new facts about his death have emerged, and senior Security Police are now being charged with his death on 24 July 1987.

Recent assassinations

Name	Organisation	Died	Perpetrator
Samuel Seliso Ndlovu	SOSCO	2/9/87	unknown
Sicelo Dhlomo	DPSC, SOSCO	24/1/88	unknown
Linda Brakvis	UDF	29/1/88	unknown
Pearl Tshabalala	UDF	10/2/88	unknown
Amos Boshomane	SEAWU	25/2/88	unknown
Nomsa Nduna	mother of unionist	6/3/88	unknown
Michael Banda	POTWA	1/7/88	unknown
Sidney Msibi	ex-ANC	5/7/88	unknown
David Webster	DPSC	1/5/89	unknown

Human Rights Commission
Five Freedoms Forum

Conclusion

This section has attempted to draw together all the varieties of means used to neutralise or eradicate political activity that is opposed to apartheid. They should be seen as adjuncts, albeit very important ones, to other forms of repression in South Africa – legislation against political opposition, bannings, restrictions and the detention of opponents.

5. 'Winning hearts and minds'

'There can be no security without reform.' This was the slogan of the P.W. Botha government in the early 1980s and it neatly summed up the intentions of the 'total strategy' reforms of the period. But the failure of those reforms to meet black political aspirations in any way and the threat of the 'people's power' uprising from 1984 to 1986 have led the state to adopt a new set of more thorough-going and militarily informed strategies, known as 'counter-revolutionary warfare'.

The essence of the new counter-revolutionary policies has often been expressed by Law and Order Minister Adriaan Vlok. To defeat the 'revolution', he says, the state must do three things:
- address the security situation (State of Emergency)
- address grievances and bring good government to the ordinary person (upgrading and municipal elections)
- address the political question (the National Council, with limited black representation).

The National Security Management System, with its 500-odd Joint Management Centres (JMCs), is the key co-ordinating structure in the implementation of this new strategy. It is designed, in the words of police counter-insurgency chief Bert Wandrag, to 'nip the revolution in the bud'. But the government's secretive network is struggling to fulfil the intentions of state security planners.

JMCs fall under the jurisdiction of the secretive 'super-cabinet' – the State Security Council (SSC) – and are the regional, district and local extensions of the National Security Management System. According to the generals and police chiefs who set them up, they are supposed to co-ordinate the counter-revolutionary warfare strategy of 'eliminating' activists and 'winning hearts and minds' of the masses ('WHAM') which

---

TROJAN HORSE

'To prevent [a] crisis, you will find the army, the police, and the JMC will co-operate.' – *SSC member*

'There is no denying a lot of influence is created by the military, because we military people are in the system and we are very proud of it.' – *NSMS (National Security Management System) official*

'In Brazil the military was careful not to dismantle the public institutions of civil government. These were kept largely intact in order to maintain the illusion of democratic government.' – *Academic*

'The NSMS, being primarily the creation of the police and security forces, is a sort of creeping coup d'etat by consent, in which accountable politicians have abrogated their power to non-accountable members of the security forces.' – *Helen Suzman MP*

---

has been put into action since 1986. But the growing economic crisis, increasing expenditure on the instruments of repression, the illegitimacy of minority rule and the depth of black political resistance are proving to be insurmountable obstacles to the 'crush – create – co-opt – reform' strategy of the National Party state.

It is in the make-up of a JMC that the overall intentions of the new security-managed policies can best be found. A JMC has five committees: Intelligence, Security, Welfare, Communications and an Executive Committee that brings together representatives of each of the four functional committees. The committees are known by their Afrikaans acronyms: GIK (Gesamentlike Intelligensie Komitee – intelligence), Veikom (Veiligheids Komitee – security), Semkom (Staatkundige, Ekonomiese en Maatskaplike Komitee – welfare), and Komkom (Kommunikasie Komitee – communications).

The Intelligence Committee is staffed by the National Intelligence Service (NIS), the security branch of the South African Police and Military Intelligence. It collects two broad kinds of intelligence on communities. The first is 'hard' intelligence on the intentions, plans, activities and problems of activists and their organisations. This intelligence is then channelled to the Security Committee. A second kind of intelligence, so-called 'soft' intelligence, encompasses the universe of attitudes, grievances and perspectives which make up a community's overall stance toward the state, its officials and its reform programme. This intelligence is sent to the Welfare Committee.

The functions of the Security Committee and the Welfare Committee encapsulate the overall intentions of state security strategists. These are, to use the words of Law and Order Minister Vlok, to 'take out' activists while 'addressing grievances'. Thereby, it is hoped, the conditions will have been laid for eventual political reform through a new accommodating local leadership and the hearts and minds of the masses will be won over to the state instead of the 'revolutionaries'.

The Security Committee, which is staffed by riot police, security police, soldiers and officers of the municipal police and kitskonstabels ('instant police'), is the repressive arm of the system. It co-ordinates the process of detentions, restrictions, bannings, spying, monitoring and allegedly also the violent attacks and harassment made on those seen to represent an extra-parliamentary threat to the state. The Welfare Committee, on the other hand, takes responsibility for co-ordinating the functions of the civilian administration. In areas identified as important to the counter-revolutionary effort, in particular education and local upgrade programmes, it will help cut red tape and ensure that things get done. Its membership consists of officials of the non-security state departments such as roads, education, welfare, manpower and health as well as local and regional officials of the provincial administrations and Regional Services Councils (RSCs).

This overall Security Management strategy is sold to the public via the fourth of the JMC's committees, Komkom. Staffed by local representatives of the Bureau for Information, plus public relations personnel from government departments, Komkom attempts to ensure the maximum publicity for welfare-type projects and government-supported 'counter-organisations' (such as youth groups, gospel associations, sports bodies, and local authorities), while explaining the sincerity of state reforms by means of letters, pamphlets, film, radio, television, newspapers, meetings and organised tours, etc.

Business involvement in the JMC strategy comes essentially through its central role in the privatisation and upgrading effort. In addition, JMCs have established so-called Community Liaison Forums and Joint Liaison Committees for the purposes of private sector liaison. Many businesses and civic and welfare-type organisations that have participated in these bodies have been unaware of the full ramifications of their involvement. Although government ministers have several times stated in parliament that the system is not secret, they have certainly not gone out of their way to make its workings public. This has led opposition politicians and academic observers to allege that it has become a 'shadow state' unaccountable to elected officials. What cannot be disputed is that the National Security Management System (which constitutionally has no status) has effectively appropriated many executive and decision-making powers for itself and is able to lean heavily on departmental officials to implement policies determined within the security-dominated JMCs.

Any assessment of the 'counter-revolutionary warfare' strategies of the JMCs must deal with the important question of whether the techniques of this kind of 20th century warfare can deal with the immensity of the problems and the political basis of the South African conflict. Any dispassionate analysis must conclude that, on present indications, they cannot.

In increasing isolation, South Africa's economy simply cannot meet the demands of the backlog in services, education, housing and jobs that apartheid has caused, let alone the future demands of the rapidly growing population. Thus the highly publicised township upgrade programme is having a major effect in no more than three or four townships around the country. Yet even if the state and the economy were able to meet the demands that have accumulated over the last 40 years, there is no evidence that a more materially comfortable population would forget that it lacks political representation. The converse may in fact be true – that as certain communities receive the benefits of upgrade programmes, the absence of political rights may be felt more keenly.

This is made all the more true by the fact that no-one understands where government policy is going. It is very difficult to 'win hearts and minds' for the incomprehensible and exclusive constitution which the National Party imposed in 1984 or for the unknown schemes of the future. Winning hearts and minds is not made any easier by the state's continuing reliance on collaborators who are very widely discredited in black communities. Too many candidates for co-option are unrepresentative individuals who take advantage of apartheid structures because 'there's money in that system'.

Meanwhile, mass democratic organisation, although weakened by the State of Emergency, still wields immense power in black communities, as evidenced by the huge three-day general strike in 1988, and the generally poor turnout for the October 1988 municipal elections. Authoritative surveys of political attitudes continue to record predominant black support for Nelson Mandela and the non-racial, democratic ideals of the ANC and the UDF.

Support for moderate black leaders such as Chief Minister Buthelezi is on a continuing downward slide – even in Durban surveys now show him coming in third behind Mandela and P.W. Botha. This political ferment will continue to grow despite scattered upgrading, continued repression and the costly promotion of moderate and conservative black leaders who have few followers.

Although the JMCs and the National Security Management System can probably keep the lid on real political change for some time to come, this will be at the expense of peace and development for all South Africans. Far from resolving anything, nearly three years of emergency have seen the country slip deeper into crisis, while expenditure on the police and army have grown more rapidly than ever before. Two alternative responses have presented themselves. On the one side is deepening impoverishment due to isolation and the corruption of long-term political stalemate. This is the 'crisis management' strategy implemented by the JMCs. But the structural crisis caused by the exclusion of the majority race from government has really become too acute to manage for much longer. The alternative would therefore be to emphasise the importance of the option for democracy. Unlike the present policy, its primary concern would be with resolving, rather than simply managing the crisis. This would involve addressing the political demands of the democratic movement.

REGIONAL SERVICE COUNCILS

All the local authorities, black, coloured, Indian and white, are represented on a Regional Services Council (RSC).

The money for the RSCs comes from levies paid by businesses on turnover and wages.

The RSC is supposed to transfer wealth (money) from the rich white towns to the poorer black ones and to help black councils by paying for things like roads, main water pipes, main electricity works, and so on.

But on a RSC, the white councils control the voting power. It is the white councils which decide how much of the money collected by the RSC will be spent in the black areas.

If a white council refuses to spend the money in this way, the black councils have no power to force it to do so. This means that a black council is dependent on the willingness of white councils to give them money.

If the money is not given, the black council remains dependent on rents, service charges and levies imposed on the people for its income. That means that rents will go on going up or that the local authority will not be able to provide the services which people need.

'You and your local authority' – Black Sash 1988

---

6. Censorship

Freedom of expression is an indispensable component of democratic government. The free flow of information is necessary to enable citizens to make informed decisions about their lives. Individuals who are deliberately kept ignorant of events and opinions and who are forced to rely upon 'official' or 'authorised' news are precluded from discovering the truth. It is precisely because South Africa is not a democracy that successive governments have found it necessary to impose severe restraints on the freedom of expression.

The pervasive system of censorship in South Africa goes far beyond the mere banning of books and films. It extends to official decisions as to what may or may not be taught in schools, to the inclusion and omission of news items by the media and to a wide range of legal constraints which ensure that certain facts and ideas are never published or ventilated. Broadly viewed, censorship serves to eliminate the propagation of information and ideas in order to control and suppress the articulation of opposition.

Legislation

Censorship laws fall broadly into two categories: those that provide for the direct imposition of censorship by outright banning; and those that inhibit or restrict what may be published. Significantly, it is the activities of society's most important institutions such as the police, prisons services and defence force that are shielded from public scrutiny by special censorship laws. Despite a permanent arsenal of an estimated 100 laws that impinge upon the free flow of information, fresh news curbs were introduced with the various States of Emergency declared every year since 1985. Apart from bans on publication of a wide range of matters, direct powers of censorship under the Emergency have been placed in the hands of state officials whose actions

A journalist protests against harsh media curbs introduced by Home Affairs Minister Stoffel Botha

Eric Miller, Afrapix

are effectively immune from judicial control. These powers have been exercised to seize and close down newspapers. Other newspapers and publications exist under the constant threat of closure. Emergency powers serve only to supplement but not replace the permanent laws. Under the permanent laws, thousands of books and publications have been banned over the past 25 years. Many of these have been prohibited for allegedly posing a threat to the security of the state (e.g., the film 'Cry Freedom' was seized by police the day it was found not to be offensive by the censorship appeal board).

Censorship is also effected by the banning of individuals and organisations both under the permanent laws and in terms of the emergency regulations. Under the latter, virtually all black extra-parliamentary movements (including the United Democratic Front and some of its major affiliates as well as the Azanian Peoples' Organisation) have been prohibited from 'carrying on or performing any activities or acts whatsoever'.

The precious right to assemble peacefully together in protest, generally recognised as an essential adjunct to the freedom of expression, has been impotent for more than a decade. Since 1976 there has been a nationwide prohibition on outdoor gatherings. Emergency powers have extended this prohibition to ban a number of indoor gatherings.

Conclusion

Perhaps the greatest tragedy of censorship in South Africa is that it has bred ignorance. The nature of the divisions in society created by the system of race classification and segregation has forced black and white South Africans to live in worlds apart. Whites tend to be ill informed about black opinion and black aspirations for a different society. Censorship also operates to shield white South Africans from many of the unpleasant truths about the conditions under which the majority of the population is living. Censorship also serves to preserve prejudices, myths and misconceptions that have been nurtured over many decades.

It is doubtful whether drastic restrictions on the freedom of speech and association will be conducive to lasting peace and good order. The opposite may well be true. As the avenues of peaceful protest are cut off, the danger increases that opposition will find violent expression.

UN Declaration of Human Rights

Article 19: Everyone has the right to freedom of opinion and expression; this right includes freedoms to hold opinions without interference and to seek, receive and impart information and ideas through any media and regardless of frontiers.

---

7. Human rights in the homelands

The patchwork of land pieces that make up the ten African homelands in South Africa – four 'independent', the other six self-governing – is one of the lynchpins of apartheid policy. Some 13 million people – more than half of South Africa's population – are resident in these areas, which cover 13.6% of South Africa. Along with the provinces, the homeland governments serve as second-tier regional administrations. The government originally planned the homelands as its solution to the problem of political accommodation of the African people – who have no vote in the central parliament of the land but only the right to vote in elections for the legislative or national assembly of their designated 'homeland'. More recently the government's constitutional plans have focused on accommodating sections of the African majority in central government structures in a very limited way.

The fact that so many people live in the homelands is the result of many factors, including decades of forced removals, evictions of Africans from white farms, the housing shortage in the white-designated area, and the harsh implementation of influx control laws. Homeland residents are in many respects worse off than Africans living outside the homelands.

First, there has been the deprivation of South African citizenship in the case of 'independent' homeland citizens. As the Transkei, Bophuthatswana, Venda and Ciskei ('TBVC states') became independent (in 1976, 1977, 1979 and 1981 respectively) all their citizens – an estimated eight million people – were deprived of their South African citizenship automatically, including those who did not live there. The Restoration of South African Citizenship Act of 1986 allowed TBVC citizens with a long period of permanent residence outside their designated homeland – some 1.75 million people – to apply for the

Opposition to the homelands: Residents of Braklaagte in the Western Transvaal at a meeting to oppose incorporation into Bophuthatswana.

Gill de Vlieg, Afrapix

return of their South African citizenship. Those, however, who remain stripped of their citizenship are subject to the Aliens Act of 1933, and in law are aliens in South Africa. They are exempted from visa and residence permit requirements, but the government can withdraw the exemptions at any time and arbitrarily 'deport' any community or person with TBVC citizenship to their designated homeland and refuse them entry into 'South Africa'. (This has already been done in a few cases for security reasons.) Furthermore, the policy of the Department of Manpower, according to lawyer Geoff Budlender, is that TBVC citizens losing their jobs must return to their homeland in order to claim UIF (Unemployment Insurance Fund) benefits, thereby removing themselves from the South African job market.

Second, the homelands are severely under-financed. Although each generates income of its own, the homelands are nevertheless all heavily dependent on central government financing. They are generally under-developed areas whose historical function has been, inter alia, to act as labour reserves, dumping grounds for the aged and the unemployed, and political 'home' to the African population. The boundaries of the homelands were so drawn as to exclude almost all the economic (industrial and infrastructural) resources of South Africa, e.g., cities, harbours, mines and dams. Their budgets totalled R7.65 billion in 1987/

37

88, an amount which could not meet the needs of the 13 million residents of these areas. Inadequate finance means that the homeland administrations generally provide even lower standards of services than those provided to Africans living in the non-homeland areas in sectors such as education, health, pensions and infrastructure. This is one of the reasons many communities resist incorporation into a homeland – a new state device to remove communities by redrawing boundaries.

Third, commuting distances from the homelands to jobs in white areas are in many cases extensive (the most notorious being the KwaNdebele/Pretoria journey of some three hours each way, every day).

Fourth, repression in some of the homelands has been more severe than in the rest of South Africa. Most central government legislation, including security laws, is applicable in the six non-independent homelands. (They have the power to pass legislation of their own in an increasing number of areas.) The 'independent' homelands adopted central government legislation upon their respective 'independence' dates but are entitled to amend or abolish it and pass legislation of their own on any matter. All four passed their own security acts, which are very similar to the security laws of the central government. (These are the Transkei Public Security Act of 1977, Bophuthatswana's Internal Security Act of 1979, the Ciskei's National Security Act of 1982 and Venda's Maintenance of Law and Order Act of 1985.) Their security legislation is in some cases more stringent than that of central government. Bophuthatswana's, for example, provides for the imprisonment for up to ten years of anyone who advises or encourages people to strike unlawfully, boycott classes, engage in consumer boycotts, attend a restricted funeral or engage in civil disobedience. The same penalty can be applied to anyone possessing documents encouraging any of these acts. All four have non-aggression pacts and extradition treaties with the central government and with each other. Detainees frequently appear to have been handed over from the central government to the 'independent' homelands and vice versa without extradition proceedings. Political trials are common in the 'independent' homelands which have their own supreme courts and appellate divisions. The 'independent' homelands have their own defence forces and both they and the non-independent homelands have their own police forces. These security forces are an integral part of South Africa's security structures.

In 1974 the government gave the non-independent homeland administrations the jurisdiction to order the removal of any tribe or person

They're everywhere: An SADF patrol in rural Bloedfontein, whose people are threatened with forced removal.

Gill de Vlieg, Afrapix

from one place to another within the homeland, restrict anyone to a particular place within the homeland, prohibit any organisation and prohibit the publication or dissemination of any document. Central government restraint over the exercise of these powers was removed in 1986. KwaNdebele was the first to pass legislation, in 1987, giving its minister of law and order these powers (in the KwaNdebele Public Safety Act).

Most of the ten homelands have police acts and civil defence acts of their own.

Lebowa passed an Indemnity Act in 1986 indemnifying the Lebowa administration and Lebowa police against legal proceedings arising out of the suppression of 'disorder' in the homeland in 1985/86. This act, which temporarily stalled hundreds of cases, was declared null and void by the Appellate Division in 1988. KwaNdebele passed a similar act in 1988, covering the period of widespread resistance in that territory associated with 'independence' plans.

KwaZulu passed an act on the Tracing and Detention of Offenders in 1987 which provides for 90-days detention without warrant for the purposes of interrogation of anyone suspected of having committed or having evidence about a crime.

POVERTY AND HARDSHIP

The level of poverty in the bantustans, where more than half the African population lives, has been documented in several studies that show meagre household incomes and a measure of the extent to which these incomes fall below survival levels. Thus a recent study by Simkins indicates that in 1980, 8.9 million people in the bantustans, or 81% of the population, had incomes below a harshly drawn minimum level. The extent of absolute poverty within the bantustans has been increasing since 1960, as then 250,000 people (5% of the population) were in households that had no income at all. By 1980 such poverty had grown with 1.4 million people (13% of the population) having no measurable income.

'The Cost of Apartheid', Michael Savage – Third World Quarterly

For example, in north-eastern Bophuthatswana a survey of 100 Pretoria commuters revealed that their average travel time to work was 17 hours 19 minutes, which was longer than the average time these workers spent sleeping... in total the South African economy contains over 2.2 million migrant workers who are employed and live in 'white' South Africa on a semi-permanent basis. In addition, it contains over 600,000 'commuting migrants' from the bantustans and large numbers of workers who are forced, through having to live far from their work, into becoming what could be termed 'daily migrants'. It is not unrealistic to state that approximately one out of three workers in South Africa can be classified as a migrant worker.

'The Cost of Apartheid', Michael Savage – Third World Quarterly

---

The central government's emergency regulations of June 1986 were made applicable to all six non-independent homelands. KwaNdebele gazetted expanded emergency regulations in August 1986 that are among the most severe of all the orders issued in terms of the Public Safety Act. They were withdrawn in September 1987 just before they were to be challenged in the Supreme Court, but most were reimposed a few months later. They included a 9pm to 5am curfew and forbade the presence of persons of school-going age in the area unless they were legally attending a school in the homeland.

The Transkei had a 10pm to 5am curfew in terms of its ongoing state of emergency for two years (the curfew was lifted in June 1987).

Violations of human rights in many of the homelands – torture, police brutality, arbitrary police and army shootings, detention without trial, deaths in detention and custody, and arbitrary detention and arrest – have been extensively documented. Police misconduct in some of the

---

BOPHUTHATSWANA – REPRESSION

- Although Bophuthatswana has a bill of rights, almost every constitution-ally guaranteed right in Bophuthatswana is contradicted by a provision in the homeland's Internal Security Act. It provides for detention without trial, declares meetings of more than 20 people unlawful unless authorised and provides the police with indemnity. Labour laws forbid workers employed in the homelands from belonging to South African trade unions.
- There have been horrifying allegations of torture by the homeland's police. Five detainees are reported to have died.
- 'We cannot forget what it was like living under the chains of apartheid. And although we are fortunate to find a way to be free without sanctions and violence, we know there are those who feel their freedom will not come without resorting to such methods.' – *President Lucas Mangope*

---

homelands, KwaNdebele in particular, appears more excessive than that of the South African Police (SAP) and is often less open to the checks, safeguards and public scrutiny that offer some protection to the victims of the SAP. Harassment of opposition groups by the security forces and vigilante groups – notably the Mbokotho in KwaNdebele – has been severe in some homelands.

Fifth, while some homeland/national assemblies provide a minimal right to political representation for homeland residents, this right is curtailed. All assemblies have not only elected members, but members appointed by homeland chiefs, chief ministers, etc. KwaNdebele, for example, has only 16 elected members in its 93-members assembly, while the ratio in other homelands is roughly equal. Until a successful court application in 1988, KwaNdebele women were denied the vote in the homeland. In 1987, Venda passed legislation making the homeland a one-party administration: every member of the Venda National Assembly was required to be a member of the Venda National Party. Percentage polls in homeland elections are very low.

Sixth, workers employed in concerns in the homelands, established in terms of the government's decentralisation programme, fare badly in comparison with their counterparts in white-designated areas. The right to collective bargaining, union organisation and minimum wages is severely limited in the homelands. Industries based in the homelands enjoy exemptions from minimum wage determinations applicable to industry in the rest of the country, and wages are notoriously low. Many homeland administrations are hostile to established trade unions. For example, the Ciskei banned the South African Allied Workers Union (SAAWU) in 1983, even though most of its members, who lived in the Ciskei township of Mdantsane, worked in East London. South African-based unions are not allowed to operate in Bophuthatswana in terms of its Industrial Conciliation Act. The Transkei's leader, Major General Bantu Holomisa, favours a trade union movement 'indigenous' to the Transkei and independent of the South African union movement.

Homeland residents or communities resisting incorporation into a homeland have enjoyed some relief through the courts. They have granted many interdicts for the release or protection of detainees in some homelands. In 1988 the Appellate Division also notably reversed the incorporation of the Moutse community (in the central Transvaal) into KwaNdebele and the 500,000-strong township of Botshabelo (Orange Free State) into QwaQwa. However, while the constitutional future of Moutse is the subject of a judicial commission, the government is set to pass legislation to override the Appellate Division's reversal of the Botshabelo incorporation (as well as to forestall any such future judgements). The legislation will remove the right of the courts to overturn proclamations issued by the state president in terms of the National States Constitution Act of 1971. The Braklaagte community tried unsuccessfully in 1989 to challenge its incorporation into Bophuthatswana. Residents feared losing their South African citizenship, as the Bophuthatswana administration is opposed to the concept of dual citizenship.

The Braklaagte community is the most recent victim of the violence and upheaval caused by the South African government's policy of forced incorporation. This policy of redrawing boundaries to shift land previously in South Africa into the homelands has become a common phenomenon. As community resistance and local and international pressure has forced the government to back down on its forced removal policy, forced incorporation has moved to centre stage as the new way of forcing black people to be in the homelands. Forced incorporation is a fundamentally violent policy. In the vast majority of cases, the communities being incorporated do not want to be in the homelands. The decision to include them in these areas is usually taken without consulting the people concerned. When the incorporation is finally implemented, the homeland administrations invariably feel compelled to show these communities that they have complete power over them.

BRAKLAAGTE'S 'BLOODY EASTER'

On Wednesday 22 March, a contingent of Bophuthatswana police and army personnel entered Braklaagte and set up a police camp in the middle of the village. When Braklaagte children schooling at Zeerust came home at about 6pm that evening, their schoolbus was stopped at the roadblock. They were ordered off the bus and told to stand in two lines. They were then asked one by one if they were citizens of South Africa or Bophuthatswana. Those who said they were South Africans were then beaten up by the soldiers with their rifle butts.

On Thursday night the community again gathered to discuss the situation. By this time migrant workers were arriving home for the Easter holidays and they wanted to be properly informed. The meeting was then broken up by the security forces using teargas, dogs and sjamboks.

By Good Friday, police activity had intensified. Residents were warned by police using loudhailers that they were not allowed to go near the chief's house. At about 10 that morning, the acting chief, Pupsey Sebogodi, was detained under section 50 of the Bophuthatswana Internal Security Act. The same morning the secretary of the local youth club was arrested with a list of youth club members. The police have since been hunting for all the people on this list. They are also looking for the tribe's elders – many of them men in their late 70s. Many people have fled the area or are hiding in the bushes.

... The people who were arrested were taken to Motswedi police station and held in terms of the Criminal Procedure Act. Attorneys acting for the community were refused access to these people on Sunday afternoon, 26 March.

... On Monday 27 March the community's attorneys again tried to see their clients. By this time they had a list of over 100 names of arrested people. Despite the fact that the Criminal Procedures Act gives people right of access to an attorney from the time of their arrest, access was refused by the police officers present on the basis that they had been given orders 'from above' and from Mmabatho that they should not allow anyone to see the Braklaagte prisoners.

The next day, as a result of intense pressure by the community's lawyers, 65 people were charged in the Lehurutse magistrate's court with public violence, arson and malicious injury to property. Acting chief Pupsey Sebogodi is number one accused. George Mogosi was also charged, but he had been hospitalised and did not appear in court. Twenty-three people were released on free bail. These were youths under 18 years and women. The rest are to appear again on Monday April 3.

The following day the lawyers returned to Motswedi police station in the belief that they would now be able to see their clients. However, they were told that there were 'orders from Mmabatho' that they were not to be given access to their clients, or to Braklaagte itself. They were told that there was no access to Braklaagte for any non-resident and that the relatives of the prisoners would be refused access.

A few days later... members of the legal team took statements from the 23 people who had been released on free bail. Amongst them were youths who had been beaten up at the roadblock the previous Wednesday, and people who had witnessed the incidents... Amongst other tortures they had been watered with a fire hose, sjambokked, forced to frog-jump, been punched and beaten with leather belts, policemen had jumped on their backs and stomachs, their legs had been pinched with pliers, and they had gone without food for long periods.

... We do not believe that access for the lawyers will spell the end of Braklaagte's troubles. Years of experience of these situations shows that once the immediate crisis is over, if decisive action is not taken to resolve the situation, violence and conflict continue with the resultant destabilisation of the entire area...

... It is only the reversal of the incorporation that will bring things back to normal.

TRAC statement on recent events at Braklaagte – 31 March 1989

8. Land and homelessness

Homelessness is arguably the most critical socio-political problem at the present time in South Africa. It is the direct result of apartheid policies and proper solutions will not be possible until apartheid laws are a thing of the past. Even then vast resources will be required to ensure that all South Africans have adequate shelter.

Estimates of the number of people who are without adequate shelter vary from six to eight million, that is at least one in every six South Africans. The greatest concentration of homeless people are in the metropolitan centres, as is to be expected, but the homelands and rural areas also have many thousands of families who are landless, homeless and dispossessed.

Many white South Africans claim that the situation has been caused by the abolition of influx control in 1986. The removal of the pass laws allowed people to move to town for the first time without having permission to do so, but it is not true that the urban homeless are recent arrivals in the cities. Influx control legislation did not stop people coming to town. They came anyway in the search for economic survival and, in spite of constant arrest and imprisonment, they stayed. In a thorough survey done by the Black Sash at Weiler's farm to the south of Johannesburg, it was found that 63% of the residents had lived in the area for more than 15 years and of these 24% were born in the area. Only 15% had been in the area for less than five years. The reasons people came to this 'squatter' settlement were varied, but all rooted in government policies. Some were squeezed off the land as white urban development took place, some came from areas that had been set aside for coloured and Indian townships, some – pushed out by overcrowding and the impossibility of finding a place to stay in the few areas set aside for black residence – came from the black townships and some had been evicted from farms, even though their families might have lived there for generations. Communities such as that at Weiler's farm exist all over the country. Their shelters are often demolished by the police. The people are arrested and charged with trespass or illegal squatting, but they continually rebuild in the same place or in the vicinity because they have no alternative.

Apart from those living in recognisable communities and settlements, thousands of individuals and small groups live where they can without even rudimentary shelter. They settle in the parks, golf courses and backyards of white city suburbs, under freeways and in doorways in the city centres, in public lavatories and railway station waiting rooms. These people are labelled 'vagrants' but most of them are not. Many of them are working men and women who have no place to stay. Thousands more domestic, farm and other workers are trapped in ill-paid and exploitative jobs just because there is a room to live in.

The causes

1. Most of the homeless in South Africa are black and have no vote for the central parliament. They can have no direct influence on the decisions made by parliament and no control over the disposition of the national wealth in the annual budget. The vote they are permitted to exercise for black local authorities or homeland governments is of no use because control of money and land rests in the white house of parliament. The only power they can exercise is the power of extra-parliamentary organisation and civil disobedience.

2. In South Africa all land is basically white and reserved for white occupation. In 1913 the Natives Land Act set aside 7% of the total land area of the country for black occupation – the reserves. In 1936 this percentage was increased to 13.6% of the total area and remains at that level. That is the total land area of the ten homelands. In addition, parcels of land have been set aside for coloured and indian occupation in terms of the Group Areas Act and there are other parcels of land for black urban residential areas. No land can be used for black occupation unless it has been so designated by the white government.

There is no solution to black homelessness without land. No self-help initiatives, private development, church or NGO planning can begin to alleviate the problem without the freeing of the land.

We need to be aware that the present distribution of land is so distorted that under any future government there will have to be massive state intervention if there is to be justice. Free market principles will not address the problem. If it is left to that it will only mean that the wealthy

Back home: A squatter returning to Noordhoek rebuilds his shack after a court declared squatters had been evicted illegally.

Eric Miller, Afrapix

of whatever colour will be able to purchase land and the poor will not benefit.

3. For more than three decades housing policies have been designed to further the exclusion of black people from common society in the pursuit of the apartheid ideology.

In the 1950s freehold titles were taken away from those few black persons who had title deeds in the urban areas. A policy of urban removal was instituted whereby black residential areas were moved further and further away from the cities and towns. The destruction of Sophiatown was perhaps the best known example in the 50s, when the residents were moved to the beginnings of what is now Soweto, their houses razed to the ground and the white suburb of Triomf established. That destruction has continued and even now the people of Oukasie at Brits are being removed to Lethlabile, 25 kms further away from the town where they work and shop because white people have moved nearer and covet their land.

PEOPLE NOT STATISTICS

- Since the Group Areas Act came into operation, 66% of families moved have been coloured, 32% Indian and 2% white. More than 126,000 families (600,000 people) were moved between 1950 and 1984.

- A young African lawyer described how he was hounded from office to office, because of the Group Areas Act, when he tried to set up a practice in Potgietersrus. He said that as soon as he found new premises the town council would pressurise his landlord to evict him.

- A white man was convicted under the Group Areas Act for living with his coloured common-law wife of 12 years in the 'white' area of Maitland, Cape Town. The magistrate warned him that he had to apply for permission for his wife and three children to live with him. Permit forms require the applicant to state whether neighbours support or object to the application. The man was charged, originally, because two of the family's neighbours complained.

- A white Villlersdorp man, who married a coloured woman, was told by the government that he had forfeited his right to be white and must move to a coloured area. The couple decided to marry after the scrapping of the Mixed Marriages Act. Section 12 of the Group Areas Act determines that when people of different races marry, they are both regarded as belonging to the race group of the male partner. When one of the partners is white, however, they are both regarded as belonging to the race other than white.

'With regard to the removal of Oukasie, Minister Heunis had claimed it was due to "poor health conditions... and because upgrading of Oukasie will prove more costly than relocating its residents". TRAC (Transvaal Rural Action Committee) disputed Mr Heunis's claim... and cited the estimates of professional consultants who said that the upgrading would cost in the vicinity of R3m. Although the cost of establishing Lethlabile was not disclosed by the government, TRAC said the provision of water alone cost R9m. The Brits Action Committee said the "real reason" for the removal was to appease the conservative white voters living in Brits.'

Race Relations Survey 1987/88

The people of Koster have to move from their old established place over the hill out of sight of the encroaching white area. Everywhere, if there is any provision for new black townships it is further and further away from where people need and want to be – Khayelitsha in the dunes

Homeless: Crossroads during 1985 meant barbed wire fences, poor drainage and ramshackle houses.

Anna Zieminski, Afrapix

far from the Cape Town city centre, Motherwell at Port Elizabeth, Botshabelo (Onverwacht) 53 kms from Bloemfontein. It must be noted that all these three places have been established in the so-called reform era.

After freehold title was abolished in the 50s a system of home ownership on a 30-year lease was substituted. Even this was abolished in 1968 after Dr Verwoerd announced the new housing policy – that there was to be no more building of family housing for black people in the urban areas. Family housing was to be built in the homelands and only hostel accommodation for migrant workers was to be allowed in the urban areas.

For the next ten years, existing housing stock became more and more crowded. Children grew up and married and another generation of children were born into already overcrowded homes. One man described the plight of the majority when he related how, when he came home from work in the evening, he could not put his feet on the floor because there were children and adolescents and middle aged aunts sleeping on the floor, under the kitchen table, and between the beds.

The South African Institute of Race Relations reported in 1987 that the average space in black areas is 3 square metres per person – that is housed people and does not include the homeless.

'The average housed urban African or coloured in South Africa thus lives in a space not much larger than a double bed. This is not including squatters and shanty dwellers, of whom there are several million.'

SAIRR Topical briefing, 6 May 1987

4. In 1978, following the 1976 Soweto revolt there was a reversal of the Verwoerdian policies. 'Orderly urbanisation' became the catch phrase. Great improvements have been made. The 99-year leasehold title was introduced and has been followed more recently by the reintroduction of freehold title for black persons in the urban areas. Secure title means that financial institutions were able to lend money to individuals who wished to buy or build private dwellings.

Large companies have been able to institute housing schemes for their employees. Township developers have been able to move into the black housing market where good profits are to be made at a time when the white housing market is becoming saturated.

But none of this is addressing the problems of the vast majority of homeless people. They simply cannot afford to benefit from this 'reform' process which is designed for political reasons to 'build a black middle class', 'to win the hearts and minds of the people' – or WHAM as this part of the military strategy for maintaining white power is known.

'The government has for the most part pulled out of black housing provision, leaving it to the private sector. But it is simply not feasible for developers to go far enough 'down-market'... the black housing shortage (is) estimated by official sources at around 800,000 units outside the 'homelands' and by the Urban Foundation at over 1.8 million units country-wide.'

Weekly Mail, 21 October 1988

'In spite of the government subsidy for first-time buyers... an estimated 60% of families cannot afford "conventionally financed housing".'

Weekly Mail, 15 April 1988

'Most agree the only way to build houses for the poor is through mass-housing schemes – and government intervention – mass housing also requires that large chunks of land are allocated for development – something that doesn't happen at the moment.'

Weekly Mail, 21 October 1988

It is estimated that at least 60% of the homeless population of the Witwatersrand cannot afford any of the housing options presently offered. The policy now is that people must pay for essential services in housing, health care, education, etc. If they cannot pay they will not get.

In 1988 the government amended the Prevention of Illegal Squatting Act to increase greatly the penalties that can be imposed both on squatters and on landowners who permit squatting. This reversed the burden of proof and reduced the protection of the courts. Yet punishment will not make homeless people disappear.

What is required is vast tracts of land accessible to city centres and industrial areas, with subsidised services – and freedom.

UN Declaration of Human Rights

Article 17: Everyone has the right to own property alone as well as in association with others; no-one shall be arbitrarily deprived of his property.

---

9. Repression and trade unions

Trade unionists in South Africa are subject to the same kinds of repression as many other activists in this country. Many trade unionists are also active in their communities so it is often difficult to say if they are victims of state repression specifically because of trade union or community activities. However, state repression does have very specific effects on trade union organisation and a variety of repressive tactics are used.

Detentions

Detentions under both section 29 of the Internal Security Act and section 3 of the Public Safety Act (the Emergency regulations) have frequently been used against unionists. People are removed from key positions in the union or union federation for long periods of time.

Recently, however, many unionists have been released from detention, owing to the massive protest hunger strikes which swept South African prisons at the beginning of 1989. Donsie Khumalo, for example, a COSATU (Congress of South African Trade Unions) Transvaal Regional Secretary, was released from detention after a protracted hunger strike to demand his and other detainees' release. Boy Sifane of TGWU (Transport and General Workers Union – a COSATU affiliate) was in detention in the Port Elizabeth area for over a year under the Emergency Regulations and was released following a hunger strike. Sifane was the TGWU local chairperson as well as being a key shop steward in his company. He was also very involved in community activity.

These unionists are still often rendered almost ineffective in organisation because of bannings or restrictions placed on them. The restriction orders under the Public Safety Act vary in nature, but have one aim: to

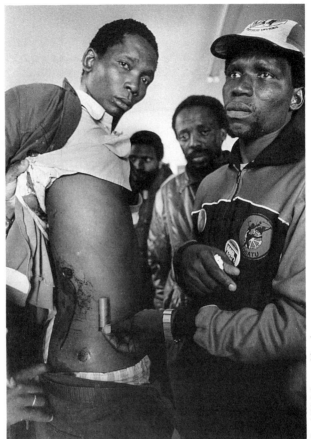

War on workers:
A mineworker
shows injuries
received during a
clash with police
at the National
Union of
Mineworkers
offices in Welkom.

Paul Weinberg, Afrapix

remove that person from effective organisation. For example, Tamsanqa
Mfazwe, the Orange Free State/Northern Cape organiser of the TGWU,
was restricted (after a period in detention) to his township of Botshabelo.
He is not able to work anywhere else and has been rendered almost
ineffective as an organiser.

Vusi Mavuso from CWIU (Chemical Workers Industrial Union – a
COSATU affiliate) was recently released from detention (he has been
detained on a number of occasions) and immediately restricted. His
restriction includes the orders that:

53

CHARGES ILL-CONSIDERED

The acquittal of Alexandra leaders on charges of treason, subversion and sedition by Mr Justice P.J. van der Walt has been hailed as a watershed judgement which may halt the steady increase in treason trials over the past ten years.

The judgement was characterised by what legal observers saw as a rebuke for attorney-generals throughout the country for pressing treason charges too readily against blacks who oppose the status quo.

The state withdrew the treason charge in the closing phases of the mammoth trial, having failed to call a single witness from the thousands of Alexandra residents to support its allegation that the five men in the dock had conspired to seize control of the township and render it ungovernable.

The judge's implicit but unmistakeable admonition to attorney-generals was: 'A charge of treason should be carefully considered and very carefully reconsidered before being brought.'

The Star, 29 April 1989

- he may not participate in the Mohlakeng Crisis Committee (Mohlakeng is his home township);
- he may not move out of the Randfontein magisterial district;
- he must be in his house at all times except for the period 8am–4pm (this is a relatively lenient restriction order – in some cases people have been restricted to their homes for all but four hours in a day);
- he may not participate in any protest against government or local authority actions or policy;
- during the period 4–7pm he must report to his local police station.

This is the government's new way of removing activists from organisation – they get the international credit for releasing detainees, but have in effect simply imprisoned people in the outside world.

Trials

The state has also harassed union leaders through long and protracted trials. This has obviously removed experienced leadership from crucial positions in the union. Moses Mayekiso, the NUMSA (National Union of Metal Workers of South Africa) General Secretary, spent six months in detention (he was detained in June 1986), was then charged with treason, sedition and subversion, and was placed on trial for two years. He was not granted bail for most of this period so could not operate in the union. His recent acquittal, a landmark judgement, raised many questions about treason trials, including the right of unionists to be involved in political struggles.

In the last two years there has also been an increasing tendency for judges to pass the death sentence on shop stewards and other union members involved in strike activity. Most of these death row sentences are murder convictions involving scabs who operated in the extremely tense strike situation, often where hundreds of workers had been dismissed. In COSATU affiliates there are shop stewards and other union members on death row from NUM (National Union of Mineworkers), CCAWUSA (Commercial Catering and Allied Workers Union), PPWAWU (Paper, Printing, Wood and Allied Workers Union), ACTWUSA (Amalgamated Clothing Textile Workers Union of South Africa) and TGWU. It is clear that judges, as state appointees, are not prepared to see the loss of the livelihood of hundreds of workers as a mitigating circumstance in such murders.

Harassment

Police involvement during industrial action has left an indelible mark on the labour movement, most notably in the killing of six SARHWU (South African Railways and Harbours Workers Union) members; six NUM members and the injuring of over 500 workers during strikes in 1987. But the trend continues, and in 1988 hundreds of striking workers, shop stewards and union organisers were arrested and released on bail of R100–R1,000 per person, thus putting an immense drain on union finances.

Striking workers find it almost impossible to hold meetings in the face of police intervention. On four occasions police broke up meetings of Soweto Council strikers and one incident led to 12 workers being hospitalised.

Besides this formal state harassment there is also the informal or vigilante type violence against union and community activists. This includes such acts as assassinations, fire-bombings of homes in townships and disappearances. All these attacks are attempts either to stop participation in organisation, or to intimidate such people from further activity often by forcing them into hiding. In March 1988 a FAWU (Food & Allied Workers Union) member, David Mofokeng, who had recently been released from detention, mysteriously disappeared. He has not been seen since. More recently, in October 1988 Siyola Mashiqana, a CWIU member, also disappeared without trace.

Unionists are also subject to constant harassment when organising rallies, conferences, seminars and so on. In September 1988 the state banned the Anti-Apartheid Conference which, on COSATU's initiative, was to bring together different anti-apartheid organisations in South Africa to discuss various key issues. More recently, a COSATU Transvaal Provincial Congress held at the University of the North was surrounded by the army and police and had to be abandoned. As far as union open-air rallies are concerned, it is almost certain that magistrates will not grant permission for these to go ahead. So all peaceful efforts at organisation and protest are banned, as a threat to the peace.

The premises of COSATU affiliates have also constantly been vandalised to prevent urgent work continuing and ensuring the loss of valuable union documents. In 1987 and 1988 respectively the head offices of NEHAWU (National Education Health and Allied Workers Union) and TGWU were completely burnt out by unknown arsonists. COSATU House, housing many unions, was destroyed by a powerful bomb in 1987, with all unions being forced to evacuate. In September 1988 the COSATU Durban Print Unit was firebombed. These are just a few examples of the on-going harassment by unknown people. The perpetrators of such deeds are never found by the South African Police or convicted in court.

Bannings

In February 1988 the state invoked the Emergency regulations to restrict COSATU's political role. COSATU, as a federation, was prohibited from releasing statements or taking any action around a number of political and economic issues stipulated by the state. The order was issued simultaneously with a banning order on 17 political, civic, youth and church organisations, leaving workers without any organised forum to defend their interests outside the employment arena. This was an attempt to confine COSATU to workplace issues alone and remove this powerful federation from the political arena. The restriction is still in operation.

Violent attacks

The situation in the Natal area needs special mention with regard to violent attacks against COSATU and other progressive organisations and

Worker power:
Workers celebrate
May Day, 1988.

Eric Miller, Afrapix

the resulting spiral of violence. Attacks by members of the Zulu cultural organisation, Inkatha, headed by the homeland leader Gatsha Buthelezi, have cost hundreds of lives – reputedly more have died in this violence than in the Beirut conflict.

Inkatha warlords, in effect, carry out the state's work by operating as an extreme right wing force opposed to change in areas like Pietermaritzburg and its surrounds and in townships like Mpopomeni where NUMSA has a stronghold. Bus drivers from TGWU in the Sizanani area have been under continual threat from Inkatha forces ever since they stayed away from work on 6 May 1987 to protest against the white elections. Inkatha youths have attacked buses causing them to career off the road, and at least four TGWU drivers have been shot and killed. COSATU members in other unions like FAWU, CWIU, NUM, and NUMSA have also suffered violent attacks from Inkatha members, resulting in severe injuries and deaths. In a number of cases the families of trade unionists have been attacked and killed.

Media

Union newsletters and pamphlets have been seized on a number of occasions, and two whole editions of 'COSATU News' were confiscated by the police – 200,000 copies per edition were taken straight from the printer. In terms of the stringent media regulations, the minister of home affairs has issued an official warning to the National Council of Trade Unions regarding its newsletter, 'Iziwlethu'. Several publications have already been banned, including particular editions of union newsletters.

Workers outside the industrial relations system

The labour movement continues the fight against certain clauses of the Labour Relations Act, but over three million workers from the most exploited sections of the working class are not even covered by the legislation. Farm workers and domestic workers are excluded from the Labour Relations Act, thus having no protection from the labour courts and no minimum standards on working conditions and wages.

Trade unions organising in these sectors face immense problems in dealing with employers who have free reign to pay starvation wages for long working hours and poor working conditions. In 1987, a large farming company, Sapekoe Tea Estate, dismissed 900 workers who were on strike and forcefully evicted them from their hostel. The company was paying an average wage of R40 a month at the time. Without even the most basic legal protection against employers, the union was not in a position adequately to defend its members. Domestic workers face a similar plight.

Passports

While South African cabinet ministers travel abroad trying to convince the outside world of their efforts to end apartheid and bring about peaceful change, trade union leaders have been refused the right even to possess a passport. The entire COSATU executive, with the exception of one person who has a Ciskeian passport, and most of the NACTU executive are without passports. Either their passports were seized by the police or their applications were turned down. In addition, a number of trade unionists have been restricted to particular magisterial districts, thus losing the freedom to travel within the country.

LAMENT

Let us speak of the wide land and the narrow strips on which we toil...

Let us speak of the dark shafts, and the cold compounds far from our families...

Let us speak of heavy labour and long hours, and of men sent home to die...

Let us speak of rich masters and poor wages...

Let us speak of freedom...

– Appeal from the labour movement of the '50s

Repressive legislation

In conclusion, special mention should be made of anti-union legislation introduced at the end of 1988. This amendment to the Labour Relations Act is a direct attack by the state on workers' right to strike and defend themselves against exploitative employers. As the International Labour Organisation accepts, workers have interests not only in pursuing better working conditions and collective work-related demands, but also in seeking solutions to economic and social policy questions. In South Africa, workers are being robbed of these rights. The amendment stipulates that:

- sympathy and solidarity strikes are against the law;
- workers cannot strike over the same issue over a period of 15 months;
- the bosses can take the union to court over an illegal strike and make it pay for losses incurred by the company during the strike – potentially destroying the union financially;
- the bosses can selectively re-employ workers after a strike;
- the bosses can easily stop a legal strike by using the courts;
- the bosses can legally dismiss a worker for no good reason in the first year of employment;
- the representative or majority union in a workplace cannot demand to negotiate for the whole workplace, so permitting the reintroduction of racist parallel unions.

Despite widespread protest, including a three-day stayaway (the biggest in South Africa) by over two million workers on each day, the state did little to accommodate workers' objections to the Labour Bill. The Labour Relations Act was promulgated in September 1988 – a sad day for the Labour Movement.

It can be seen from the above examples that the state feels free to meddle in the relationship between workers and employers. This is done in the guise of regulating labour relations through respectable government legislation, but in reality it is just another sustained attack on the growing power of workers to demand more political and economic rights in South Africa.

UN Declaration of Human Rights

Article 23: Everyone has the right to form and join trade unions for the protection of his interests.

---

10. Education for inequality

A partheid education conforms to a policy of separation, division and deliberate inequality. This policy has resulted in the terrible impoverishment of all South Africa's youth. It is a system that inculcates a sense of superiority into some, whilst denying the vast majority what is their fundamental right – an education of decent quality. All South Africans are immeasurably damaged by it.

The situation is so dynamic that any factor may trigger a new student/state confrontation and radically change the existing circumstances. Racially divided education is a time bomb ticking away in South African society.

The structure of apartheid education

There are currently 19 education departments in South Africa. Their composition is as follows:
- Five white – one National and four Provincial: Cape, Transvaal, Orange Free State and Natal
- One 'Coloured'
- One Indian
- Eleven black – one for 'South African blacks' controlled by the Department of Education and Training (DET), six in the non-independent homelands and four in the 'independent' homelands.

Amongst P.W. Botha's reform promises was a single education policy. Nothing has come of this.

Spending
The structure and spending in apartheid education speak for themselves. *The Star* (18 March 1989) gave the following figures for 1986:

Education for inequality

White education	R2,267,986,000
Black education (DET controlled)	R1,031,453,000

The amounts spent on children in different race groups in 1986/87 (most recent figures available) were as follows:

Black	R476.95*
'Coloured'	R1,020.40
Indian	R1,904.20
White	R2,508.00

* This is for DET-controlled schools – homelands have their own education budgets and spend even less per child. There is no compulsory education for black children in South Africa.

(Source: South African Institution of Race Relations 1987/88)

Thus 5.25 times more is spent per capita on a white than on a black child.

'In the Department of Education and Training school system, the government indicated that there was a shortage of 3,327 Primary School classrooms and 2,448 Secondary School classrooms in 1984. It estimated that it would cost R420 million to meet this shortfall. The shortfall could be eradicated by switching the equivalent sum paid to the South African Development Trust over the past four years, for purchasing land to consolidate black areas, to building classrooms; it could be met in one year by disengaging militarily from Namibia; it could be met in just over two years by charging 15% of the cost of their education to white pupils.

'Similarly apartheid expenditures on maintaining spare capacity in "white" educational institutions, which currently involve having over 1,035 spare places in eight "white" schools in central Cape Town alone, and 2,683 empty places in white teacher training colleges, could be abolished in one exceedingly limited step toward addressing the educational crisis upon us.'

'The Cost of Apartheid' by Michael Savage

It is patently absurd to claim, as the state does, that the phenomenon of 'separate but equal' can exist where different amounts are spent on children according to their race group. To expect the recipients of this discrimination to accept such a false premise is deeply offensive.

Repression
Repression in education was as severe as in all areas of South African life in 1988. Many students and teachers were detained. Schools were

---

WHAT STUDENTS SAY

'My name is John. I was born on 13.9.1969 in Cape Town and moved to Pietermaritzburg six years ago. I am at school at Maritzburg College and am starting Std. 10 in 1987. I am very interested in music and I play the organ and piano. I intend to study music when I have completed school.

'I joined a local campaign about a year ago and have participated in their programmes. Realising the need for justice and peace in South Africa, I became involved, and this has made clearer the injustice in South Africa. I live a peaceful, comfortable life and I object to a policy which prevents others from enjoying a life similar to mine.'

'My name is Themba. I was born in 1969. At the beginning of 1986 I was in Std. 9, and I was vice president of the SRC. My home is in X Township and I am now in hiding. My ambition is to negotiate with other political organisations. My favourite things are music and the strugle [sic].

'I was born in Pietermaritzburg in Edendale Hospital. My father works in town. I started schooling when I was five years old. I failed only Form 3. I became involved in politics in 1984 when I joined a youth organisation. I left my home in April when Inkatha members attacked my home. I am in hiding from that day. Also I was held in detention for 16 weeks. I have not been able to complete school this year. I think the best solution among black students is to get a people's education, and every problem will be solved like that.'

---

suspended or closed. Teachers and principals sympathetic to the grievances of pupils were transferred, PTSAs' (Parent/Teacher/Student Associations) and students' meetings were banned as were any discussions around the issue of alternative education, known as 'People's Education'. Many individuals and organisations were banned. This particularly affected the National Education Crisis Committee (NECC), which had continued to play a crucial role in diffusing tension and in addressing the issue of educational alternatives. Its top leadership was detained. Any local structure thought to be linked to the NECC was eliminated. Other organisations restricted included the National Education Union of South Africa (NEUSA), a non-racial body that had been actively involved in working for teacher unity. Many student organisations were restricted. Further forms of repression were the use of right wing state-supported 'vigilantes' and the instruction by the DET to principals to provide names of student activists. Students released from detention were not permitted to re-register in the schools.

'As for those students who did attend school, educationalist Ken Hartshorne said recently: "Pupils and teachers at black schools are often present in the flesh but not in spirit, because attitudes have not changed and the fundamental issues of separation, discrimination, isolation and white domination have not been addressed in an effective way."

Others say pupils, many of whom have not known a year of uninterrupted secondary education, have been harmed psychologically by the on-going conflict. Former journalist and now university teacher, Phil Mtimkulu says: "They are rootless and volatile. Any little thing that happens brings out their anger." He says there is little point in pupils going to school while there is little motivation to learn.'

Black Sash Magazine, September 1988

Black education 1988/89

The situation in black education deteriorated sharply in 1988. In many urban areas there was an almost complete breakdown of the learning environment. In order to provide a picture of the situation, regional conditions are briefly described:

Soweto
Pupils were engaged in lengthy stayaways. Several schools were closed by the Department of Education and Training (DET). A breakdown in discipline occurred, teachers were demoralised and intimidated. A high level of fear, frustration, anger and despair was felt by pupils. Conditions conducive to teaching did not exist and the SAIRR estimated that no effective teaching took place in 54 Soweto high schools. There was a strong security presence around the schools. This caused tension and anger amongst students.

Western Cape
Disintegration of education became the norm. Schools were wracked by conflict because of the DET's refusal to allow large numbers of pupils to register and because of DET's prohibition of PTSA meetings. Several teachers were suspended by the DET, causing further tensions and conflict. In July an official estimate gave a 50% attendance at schools.

Spirit of
resistance: Cape
Town students
demand an end
to harassment.

Adil Bradlow, Afrapix

Eastern Cape
Although there were no major boycotts during the year, appalling conditions existed with severe shortages of facilities. Repression was harsh and many student leaders were detained.

Natal
Serious conflict existed between Inkatha and non-Inkatha forces and the conflict spilled into the area of education. For political reasons, many pupils were not able to register. Many left Inkatha-controlled areas to seek alternative schooling elsewhere.

Matriculation results
The start of 1989 saw thousands of matriculants seeking readmission to schools after disastrous results for 1988. Regulations introduced by the DET in November 1988 included a clause that refused matriculants permission to reregister. This situation caused chaos as many thousands of students were turned away. *The New Nation* (13 April 1989) estimated that 50,000 matriculants would not be allowed to rejoin in 1989.

Summary
The situation in black schooling is near complete collapse. There is a critical shortage of teachers, schools are seriously short of facilities,

65

students and teachers continue to be detained or harassed and many thousands of children are receiving little or no education. The DET regulations issued in November 1988 are a further measure to control black schooling and prevent democratically elected PTSAs from participating in structures or formulating policy. They are another cause of great anger and tension.

White education

White children too are deprived and denied a fair and well grounded education, for they are indoctrinated with Nationalist Party ideology through the system of Christian National Education (CNE). This system entrenches the ideology of discrimination and the concept of racial superiority. it presents seriously distorted views. Very little resistance is offered by parents and educators, themselves products of this system which was introduced in the 1950s.

The policy of CNE makes no pretence of an unbiased approach. Further, the state controls white schools in a vice-like grip and white education departments fiercely guard their terrain. For example, white school principals in the Transvaal have been ordered not to allow materials produced by several human rights organisations from being circulated or discussed in their schools. Human rights organisations attempting to provide alternative points of view have been accused of trying to involve pupils in politics – a great irony, when the whole system of white education is based on a political ideology.

White children are not in any way being prepared for a post-apartheid South Africa. Instead the concept of a God-ordained superiority is reinforced, damaging the minds of all white South Africans.

Conclusion

Article 26 of the Universal Declaration of Human Rights states: '1. Everyone has the right to education... 2. Education shall be directed to the full development of the human personality and to the strengthening of respect for human rights and fundamental freedoms...'

As in all aspects of South African life, the apartheid education system is a complete denial of this fundamental human right.

In accordance with Article 26, the guidelines issued in 1988 by the African National Congress are emphatic about the need for full, equal and compulsory education for all in a post-apartheid South Africa. When a

17-year-old youth says 'I feel hopeless and helpless' and another says 'Even though I try my utmost best to pass matric I can't make it. They are keeping us out of the schools. They are keeping us in the working force', then it is time to demand the end to apartheid education. For the emancipation of all South Africans, this is essential.

Much of this information was taken from an unpublished summary, 'Trends in Black Education 1988', by V. Khanyile, Chairperson of the National Education Crisis Committee (NECC).

The UN Declaration of Human Rights

Article 26: Everyone has the right to education... Education shall be directed to the full development of the human personality and to the strengthening of respect for human rights and fundamental freedoms...

---

11. Militarisation and white South Africa

'If we saw a well-built kaffir we'd know he was a terr [terrorist]. If he had soft feet that would prove it beyond doubt, at least if we were out in the bush, because who else wears shoes? Sometimes you could also see marks on his shoulders or his waist from the webbing. We'd interrogate him, and if he was stubborn he could have trouble. Maybe we tie him to the front of the Buffel and do a little bundu-bashing. Feel it? Why should I feel it? I wasn't on the front of the Buffel. If he's still okay when we get tired of driving around maybe we give him a ratpack (a seven-day food supply) and tell him to shut up. Sometimes they shout and complain and then we have no choice, we have to finish him off. Sometimes he's finished off before we stop driving. Then we just untie him and say farewell.' (SADF soldier, Frontline, August 1985).

Many South Africans who engage in acts of cruelty are terrifyingly normal. They are people who have been socialised into conformity, into an unthinking obedience to authority, or into the belief that some human beings (Jews, 'moffies' [homosexuals], 'kaffirs', communists or whatever) are non-human and outside the boundaries which define human/humane treatment.

War toys are part of this process of socialisation. There is a connection between war toys and torture – both are symptoms of a highly militarised society.

Mobilising for war

Whether the level of militarisation is measured through military expenditure, the size and sophistication of the weapons systems, the scale of

Troops out of the townships: An elderly Soweto resident expresses her feelings.

Paul Weinberg, Afrapix

repression, or the political influence of the military, South Africa is an extremely militarised society. Indicators of this are:

- defence expenditure. In June 1987 the annual defence budget was increased by 30% to R6,686 million. And there are hidden items which make it far larger than that – almost R11 billion, according to one commentator;
- the sophistication of its weapons system;
- the progressive extension of compulsory military service for white male youths – now two years plus annual camps;
- the domination of the political system by a National Security Management System controlled by the South African Defence Force (SADF) and the South African Police (SAP);
- the local armaments industry (Armscor) is the third largest corporation in South Africa. It is the largest arms manufacturer in the southern hemisphere and the tenth largest in the world;
- increasing militarisation of white schools through cadets, youth preparedness, and veld schools in the Transvaal – where selected Transvaal Education Department teachers now carry guns;
- the rapid increase in gun sales, with one in four white South Africans now owning a gun;
- reliance on the SADF to suppress resistance in sectors as diverse as education, health and labour. The SADF has been used to break the schools boycott in Soweto, for strike breaking at Baragwanath Hospital, in evicting squatters and rent boycotters, and in the

registration and screening of students at the University of the North (Turfloop);
* a vigorous and spectacular consumerist militarism evident in war toys, games and films which glorify military encounters.

Civilians and the SADF

There is a pervasive ideology that accepts violence as the solution to conflict and problems. It involves deep acceptance of organised state violence as a legitimate response, with a glorification of war in which both actors and encounters are portrayed in heroic terms. There is an acceptance amongst the white community of the power of the military and its encroachment into civilian areas. Above all, war is viewed as 'normal'.

There are four direct and obvious points at which citizens connect to the SADF and the militarisation of society:
* as conscripts with increasing length of service and all the disruption of work, education and family relationships that prolonged separation involves. Growing periods of compulsory military service reflect increased black resistance. And the SADF relies heavily on coercion to obtain its manpower: eight out of every nine members of the SADF are Citizen Force or National Service conscripts;
* as taxpayers who are footing an enormous bill for the war in Angola. The Namibian war costs South Africa more than R2 million every day;
* as citizens increasingly ruled by an elaborate national security system and other extra-parliamentary structures shrouded in secrecy;
* as eager and active consumers of a war culture.

The high costs of militarisation

The cost of militarisation is high, both in physical and psychological terms.

There is the 'final sacrifice' paid by young South African men killed in action far from home. Professor Green of the Institute for Development Studies in Sussex has estimated that as a proportion of the white population, the number of white South Africans who have died fighting SWAPO is more than three times the number of American lives lost in Vietnam.

Increasing numbers of white South Africans are resisting military service: the numbers failing to report for duty at each call-up is now

---

WHAT DO TROOPS DO IN THE TOWNSHIPS?

Giving evidence in support of a conscientious objector, an SADF conscript described some incidents he had seen involving SADF troops in the townships:

- Using catapults with stones against residents to provoke 'action'.
- Placing a ten-year-old boy in a small 'bin' behind a Buffel. A corporal then beat the boy with a stick.
- Blackmailing shebeen owners into providing them with liquor.
- Breaking up fences for firewood.
- Meeting a congregation as they left a Sunday church service and then teargassing them.
- Hiding among township houses while a Buffel was driven about in a manner which it was hoped would provoke action.
- Assaulting residents using sticks cut from trees because troops were not issued with sjamboks.

'I asked him why he was hitting the boy. His words were "prevention is better than cure".'

Sources: Weekly Mail, 15 May 1987; Weekly Mail, 26 June 1987.

---

secret, but by all accounts it has risen very dramatically since the use of the SADF in the townships after October 1984. Growing numbers of conscripts have applied to the Board for Religious Objection. And many of South Africa's most competent and talented young men emigrate each year.

The costs of war go further than this. For many young men, their two years of military service are a psychologically disturbing experience. Research by Diane Sandler, involving case studies of soldiers who have done township duty, reveals aggressive tendencies and a deep sense of alienation and meaninglessness among these soldiers.

According to the Rev van Arkel, 'South African men – particularly Afrikaans men – have the dubious distinction of committing more family murders than men in any other society in the world.' He relates this phenomenon to 'escalation of violence at all levels of our society'.

Public and private violence

The core component of militarism is the reliance on violence as a solution to problems and conflict. Public and private spheres are connected by a war culture, which includes a central notion of security. The state claims that violence (or force) is necessary to protect state security – but this violence spirals and spreads so that many become more fearful and anxious about personal security. The war psychosis or siege mentality then creates the demand for security firms and firearms.

Secrecy and security

One of the most alarming aspects of militarism, both in South Africa and as a global phenomenon, is its secrecy. It is through secrecy, through silence – a silence which distorts and damages any attempt to gain understanding – that consent to militarism is secured.

After the October 1987 strike into Angola the minister of defence said: 'South Africa is prepared to pay the price (for freedom), and it knows the price is high.'

High levels of military spending drain resources away from urgent needs in housing, education and health. There is a clear link between high levels of military spending and poverty and deprivation elsewhere in the social order. Emigration is a further drain on the skilled person-power needed to tackle these social problems.

In social terms, a society has developed where personal relationships are fragile and family units fractured as increasing numbers of young people leave the country. In psychological terms, South African society has become a battlefield littered with the bodies of damaged people. No society can afford a price so high.

This article was adapted from a longer version appearing in 'Work in Progress' No. 53, April 1988.

12. Human rights and conscientious objection

'I want to break down barriers which divide us and reject violence as a means to do so. If I were to serve in an institution such as the SADF, which I see as perpetuating these divisions and defending an unjust system, it would be contrary to all I believe in.'

For saying and acting on these words Charles Bester (18) is serving a six-year prison sentence. David Bruce, likewise, is a prisoner for the next six years. In stating his reasons for refusing to serve in the SADF, he said:

'I feel I have no choice but to set myself against those who choose the path of increasing racial violence and racial hatred in the firmest way which is possible to me.'

Bruce and Bester, together with other objectors Ivan Toms and Saul Batzofin who have recently received prison sentences of 18 months for their refusal to serve, represent the most forceful and visible demonstration of growing resistance to military conscription in South Africa. Their heavy penalty represents the determination of the South African government to suppress this resistance.

Conscription affects all white males

Military conscription affects all white male South Africans. It was introduced in the 1960s and the length of military service has progressively increased as the South African government has faced growing resistance to apartheid.

Up until the end of 1988, conscripts had to serve an initial two-year period of service followed by shorter periods, called 'camps', usually of one to three months duration, spread over the following 12 years until a total of 720 days has been completed. This has just been altered, but with little effect:

'According to Mark Swilling, researcher at Wits University's Centre for Policy Studies, the announced reduction in the period of service will make little difference to the actual amount of time served. He cited the 1986 Defence White Paper which stated that conscripts only served an average of 50.7% of their total 720-day camp requirement – which amounts to 362 days – or an average of 30 days a year over a 12-year period. According to the new procedure conscripts will be required to serve up to 30 days a year over a 10-year period. "What has happened is that the de facto situation has now become a de jure one," he said.'

Weekly Mail, 28 April 1989

Foreign male citizens are also conscripted by means of a law that automatically makes them South African citizens if they are between the ages of 15.5 and 25 years and have been permanent residents for five years. If a foreign citizen were to renounce his South African citizenship he would almost certainly be deported.

Conscription and the law

Conscription laws in South Africa are harsh and wide-ranging. For example, it is an offence punishable by imprisonment of up to six years to encourage or aid a person not to do military service. Further, in terms of the Emergency regulations, it is an offence to 'undermine the system of compulsory military service'. Contravention of this regulation is punishable by imprisonment of up to ten years.

The primary mechanism used by the government to deal with conscientious objectors is contained in a section of the Defence Amendment Act of 1983. This prescribes that a conscript convicted of refusing to serve in the SADF must be sentenced to a compulsory prison term of one and a half times the service he owes the SADF, or 18 months, whichever is the greater. An objector who has done no military service will thus be imprisoned for six years.

This heavy penalty was imposed to counter a growing number of conscripts who were prepared to be imprisoned rather than do military service in the aftermath of the Soweto uprising in 1976. Within a few years, 12 objectors were imprisoned for periods ranging from four to 18 months.

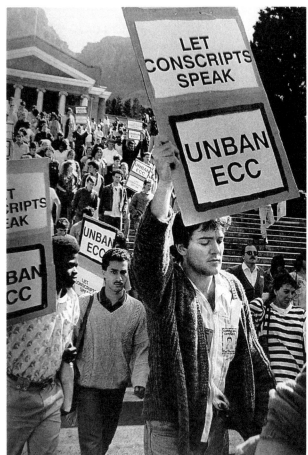

Hours after the banning of the End Conscription Campaign, students at the University of Cape Town show their displeasure.

Eric Miller, Afrapix

Conscientious objectors treated as criminals

Imprisoned objectors are regarded as common criminals by the authorities and are granted no recognition as prisoners of conscience. Nor have the authorities taken any special steps to ensure their safety. Ivan Toms was assaulted in prison by another prisoner. David Bruce has been held in a cell with an ex-policeman convicted of murder. Objectors imprisoned prior to 1983 were held with prisoners convicted of right wing violence and there were instances of assault.

END CONSCRIPTION CAMPAIGN (ECC)

ECC is a legal movement whose main aim is to campaign for a change in the law regarding compulsory military service in South Africa. ECC believes that conscripts should be given freedom of choice as to how they serve their country.

Short-term proposals include:

- Calling for conscripts to be allowed to choose not to serve in the black townships or Namibia – on similar lines to the situation in World War Two where servicemen had the right to refuse to serve outside South Africa's borders.

- Calling for all conscripts, and not only 'bona-fide religious pacifists', to be allowed to do alternative service in non-government bodies and for a period of equal duration to that of military service.

Another important aim is to oppose all expressions of militarisation in South Africa.

EEC has 52 member organisations nationally. These include religious, civil-rights, youth, women's and political organisations. It also has nine regional branches and five campus branches which involve several hundred active members. In addition, it has several thousand supporters throughout the country. Public meetings have attracted up to 4,000 people.

'The End Conscription Campaign (ECC) is a direct enemy of the South African Defence Force.' – *Minister of Defence General Magnus Malan*

Unlike common criminals, who may end up serving only a third of their sentences if granted remission and parole, objectors have thus far had to serve their full sentences.

Limited accommodation of religious objectors

The Defence Amendment Act does, however, provide a limited alternative for those who can prove to a specially constituted board that they have religious objections to serving in any armed force. Such objectors are required to perform civilian service in a government department for a period of one and a half times the total service they owe the SADF in one continuous period. If a religious objector has done no military service, he will have to serve six years civilian service. Despite the punitive length of service and low rate of pay, more than 1,200 conscripts have availed themselves of this option since 1984.

Consequences of the Defence Amendment Act

The Defence Amendment Act of 1983 initially succeeded in stopping the stream of objectors going to prison. The punitive and limited nature of the legislation, however, led to an increasing number of young white men, especially those with professional qualifications, leaving the country. The legislation also provided the impetus for the formation of the End Conscription Campaign (ECC) which highlighted the deficiencies in the law for conscientious objectors and articulated the opposition to conscription of many white South Africans.

The ECC has been targeted by the State in many ways, ranging from dirty tricks campaigns to prolonged detention of office bearers, and has now been banned.

Increasing resistance to service in the SADF

The township uprisings of 1985 and 1986, the imposition of the State of Emergency and the deployment of SADF troops in the black townships together with the escalation of the war in Angola all led to a new wave of objection.

In August 1987, 23 men in the Cape Town area made a public declaration of their refusal to do military service. Shortly afterwards, one of the '23', Dr Ivan Toms, who had already completed his initial service, was called up for a camp. He refused to serve and was sentenced. Since then, David Bruce, Charles Bester and Saul Batzofin have been tried and sentenced.

'As loyal South Africans, we wish to contribute to the building of a peaceful and just society. The SADF violently maintains a fundamentally unjust and oppressive system. We cannot make a contribution to justice and at the same time be part of the SADF.' – David Bruce

In response to these and other developments, the government banned the End Conscription Campaign by declaring it a 'restricted organisation' in September 1988. On 7 February 1989, a group of women held press conferences simultaneously in Cape Town, Durban and Johannesburg. They presented a declaration as mothers urging the institution of 'constructive, non-punitive alternatives to obligatory military service':

'Give our sons a choice
'For mothers around the country the bi-annual call-up once again highlights the moral dilemma of young men drafted into the SADF.

> *'Many young men wish to serve their country but question the role of the SADF. They ask whether the SADF presence in the townships and beyond our borders is defending the country they love or the system of apartheid, which they find indefensible. For others, the whole concept of bearing arms is abhorrent. We share their anguish and stand in support of them. We call for constructive, non-punitive alternatives to obligatory military service.*
>
> *'We are deeply aware of the traumatic effect military service has on young men. For many of whom there is little real option but to serve in the SADF. The appalling choices are a six year prison sentence, voluntary exile or the twilight world of avoidance. If they are religious pacifists they face a punishing six years of so-called community service, often in meaningless jobs not necessarily utilising their skills. We support them all whatever their decision.*
>
> *'Instead of our young men being embroiled in moral conflict, civil strife, fear and violence we want them to have the choice of serving in other ways. Without this choice South Africa loses their skills and contribution to a free, open and peaceful future for all.*
>
> *'We cannot afford this loss.'*

Conclusion

No-one should be forced to defend apartheid. However, the South African government has thus far given no indication that it intends providing a non-military alternative to those who object to serving in the SADF because they regard it as defending an unjust system. Until they do, opposition to conscription will continue to grow.

13. Destabilisation in Southern Africa

South Africa is waging a full-scale war against its neighbours. Action is not limited to isolated commando raids. South Africa also directly supports surrogate armies in at least five of the neighbouring states. The war is hidden and diffuse, but the cost is massive. Because of South African actions, more than 900,000 people have died since the beginning of 1980. The material cost is at least $35 billion (R70 bn).

Joe Hanlon
Mark Orkin (ed) 'Sanctions against Apartheid'

W e can distinguish three different interpretations of the term 'destabilisation' in the South African context:

- The South African government considers its policy to be a stabilisation policy. Opposition and resistance against the South African minority regime is interpreted as destabilisation.
- In terms of political and economic analysis, destabilisation describes the planned, deliberate and systematic actions of the South African government as hostile intent against the neighbouring countries of South Africa. It makes their national reconstruction impossible and intensifies their dependence on the South African regime, thereby neutralising their resistance to the apartheid system. Such a destabilisation policy relies on methods of economic pressure or economic aid, on military or police incursions into neighbouring countries, and on direct or indirect support to resistance movements operating in these countries against their governments.
- In a more comprehensive usage of the term, destabilisation applies to the internal policy of the South African government as well as to the external destabilisation policy directed against neighbouring coun-

tries. Since the beginning of the 1970s, the South African government has found it impossible to contain the intensifying resistance of the majority of economically and politically dispossessed people. It has responded to the pressure by defusing, diverting and repressing resistance with a variety of measures such as the creation of homelands, the 1983/84 constitution of the Republic of South Africa with the tricameral parliament, the state of emergency, the use of vigilantes to eliminate political opponents, the erosion of juridical procedures, restriction of the press, deliberate use of the media for disinformation, and an indirect support of divisive evangelistic movements attacking the South African churches because of their resistance to the apartheid system. In the comprehensive sense, internal and external destabilisation are dimensions of one and the same destabilisation policy.

The internal dimension of the destabilisation policy (reform and repression) and the external dimension (military or police incursions, hit squad murders and offers of economic aid) are not contradictory but complementary methods of one and the same destabilisation policy. Shifts in the methods used occur in response to the shifting influence of rival pressure groups within the South African government or the National Party, varying international pressures and changing levels of resistance within South Africa.

The root cause of instability in the Southern African region is the minority regime of the Republic of South Africa and its refusal to comply with generally accepted principles of justice.

Western influence

The destabilisation policy of the South African government receives considerable support from destabilising trends in the traditions and economic policies of Western countries such as:

- the use of technology for their economic benefit with no consideration of the needs of the human community as a whole and no consideration of responsible stewardship over natural resources;
- a concept of development based on hidden racist assumptions and faith in economic growth and the self-regulating forces of the world market, irrespective of the local context and the needs of the local population, resulting in the destruction of subsistence economies;
- the granting of development aid for minority projects in the Third World and the insistence on repayments of loans with high interest

Get out of
Angola: Black
Sash protestors
at a picket in
Cape Town.

Jonathan Kaplan, Afrapix

rates disrupts social structures and social services, erodes democratic
structures and results in the establishment of authoritarian regimes.
The security of the state is emphasised and any resistance on the part
of masses of the people is repressed;

• the promotion of the national security ideology and the support of
military regimes.

Legitimacy and destabilisation

The policy of the South African government is in principle a destabilisation policy that results from its legitimacy crisis. The South African
government does not dare to test its policies by holding free elections in
an undivided South Africa. It is not committed to generally accepted
principles of justice when it feels its interests to be threatened.

From the perspective of the South African government, a destabilisation policy is indispensable in order to maintain its regime. Recent events
and agreements reached in the negotiations concerning Namibian
independence, the war in Angola and the reduction in support to
Renamo in Mozambique do not indicate that the South African govern-

81

ment has abandoned its destabilisation policy. It is a shift in stategy due to military, economic and political pressures such as the military defeat in Angola, the inability of the South African economy to sustain the expenses of the war in Angola, the initiative of the Soviet Union to defuse tensions in international crisis areas and the impact of this initiative on the United States.

For most people living in the southern African countries, this shift in the strategy of the South African government signifies progress, because it has the potential to reduce the terrible loss of life and because it offers the opportunity of stabilising life in these areas. Nevertheless, this shift in strategy does not yet promise any possibility of life being stabilised in South Africa itself.

14. The cost of apartheid

An examination of how South Africa channels its resources reveals much about the shaping of South African society and its priorities. In allocating public funds to existing educational, health or economic programmes, conscious decisions have been made to support selected policies. These decisions determine the degree to which any group of people have access to health, education and the basic necessities of life such as food, housing and employment.

At one level, to examine the economic cost of the apartheid system is to engage in a narrow book-keeping exercise, albeit one fraught with very considerable difficulties. However, at a more important level, attempts to assess the cost of apartheid provide an indication of the economic resources that this policy consumes. Were apartheid not to exist, these are the funds that could be used to help reconstruct South African society along non-racial, democratic and more equitable lines. The costs of reconstructing the basic social institutions along such lines will be enormous and some gauge of the resources available should be attempted.

On costing apartheid

Apartheid's structures permeate the whole of society. An indication of the extent to which this is so can be made by identifying seven areas of its cost.

First, there are direct costs involved in implementing and maintaining apartheid programmes. These costs include supporting ten 'homeland' governments, providing duplicated services in areas such as health and education, carrying out black population removals from 'white' areas, and implementing Group Areas legislation.

Second, there are indirect costs involved in implementing apartheid, which again are enormously varied. These include capital expenditure

83

on buildings used in carrying out the policy, on transport systems needed to accord with territorial segregation, and on the vehicles, machinery and communications used in implementing the system.

Third, there are enforcement costs involved in applying and policing apartheid. Police, courts, magistrates, prisons, officials and the Defence Force are all involved to greater and lesser degrees in enforcing the policy of apartheid. In addition there are the costs paid by those on the receiving end of apartheid – those, for example, who have to spend time in courts and prisons because of apartheid legislation.

Fourth, there are lost opportunity costs arising from apartheid. These are substantial and involve the loss of foreign investment and the consequent lower rates of economic growth. As a result of apartheid, artificial limitations are placed on the use of economic and human resources which result in the loss of potential skills and economic growth.

Fifth, there are punitive costs of apartheid flowing from embargoes and sanctions. These directly involve the loss of trade but also involve premiums that South Africa has to pay to obtain key materials such as oil, also the costs of stockpiling these materials and attempting to become self-sufficient in the production of them.

Sixth, and most important, there are the human costs of the apartheid system. These are enormous, involving suffering and brutality in the lives of large numbers of South Africans as a direct result of apartheid policies. Some of these costs can be seen in the prisons, townships and rural areas of South Africa but most are to be viewed within the daily fabric of South African life.

Seventh, there are regional costs, paid by South Africa's neighbours in increased military expenditures due to apartheid policies, direct war damage, lost exports and lost economic growth.

There is a problem in disaggregating the cost of apartheid policies from the cost of providing those services that would be supplied by any non-apartheid state. While the South African budget reveals some of the direct costs of implementing apartheid policies, the bulk of them are hidden from immediate view. Thus, for example, the 1985/6 budget indicates that over R10 million was allocated directly for forced removals of blacks from white areas. This cost can only be a partial one, for not only does it exclude the considerable individual expenses faced by the people removed but it takes no account of such items as the salaries of officials implementing this policy, the capital expenditure on machinery

A call for sanctions: A crowd supporting Bishop Desmond Tutu says sanctions will do less harm than apartheid.

Zubeida Vallie

and buildings used in population removals, nor the costs of the legal and judicial apparatus of the state that underpin these removals.

Another difficulty in costing apartheid is the impossibility of pinning down the individual costs of the human suffering, humiliation and anger that occur as a result of this policy. Some estimates of the economic costs that individuals face as a result of removals under the Group Areas Act, or imprisonment under discriminatory statutes, may be arrived at, but such figures reflect only faintly the appalling toll that apartheid exacts on its victims.

The current costs of apartheid

One can begin by providing an estimate of the impact of lost opportunity costs on rates of economic growth. There can be no doubt that the South African economic growth rate had severe internal restraints placed on it due to restrictive racial legislation and the international actions against apartheid. In terms of economic growth it is not unreasonable to assume that had apartheid not existed, the real Gross Domestic Product over the period 1980-1985, instead of increasing by 1.1%, would have increased by an additional 2.5% per annum to provide an annual growth of 3.6% in GDP over this six-year period. This assumption is based on the growth rates experienced by semi-developed countries over the period and an estimate made in the last Economic Development Programme that South Africa should experience a 3.6% rate of economic growth.

This cost will undoubtedly increase in future as the withdrawal of foreign investment escalates and further sanctions are imposed. In an economy extensively involved in foreign trade – for example, last year its exports represented the equivalent of 34% of GDP and its imports some 23% – it is inevitable that international actions against the policies of South Africa will have a considerable impact on its economic growth rate. The cost of apartheid in terms of lost economic growth is likely to expand greatly in the immediate future.

A second economic indicator of the cost of the apartheid policy is South Africa's Gross National Product. The most significant past estimate of the effect of apartheid on economic output was made by a prominent businessman, Mr L G Abrahamse, in 1977. Whilst adopting what he termed a very conservative approach, he stated that 'on the assumption that over the past 30 years there had been natural integration on the economic front instead of segregation' and 'a consequent elimination of such factors as wasteful expenditure aimed at segregation and higher levels of labour utilisation, labour skills and investment' then 'it would not be unreasonable to assume that GNP per capita would have been some 50% higher'. He concluded that 'on this very conservative basis' for the year 1976, the cost of apartheid was R13,000 million. One can update this calculation and, using the same 'conservative' assumption that GNP would be 50% higher without apartheid, it can then be concluded that in 1985 apartheid cost South Africa over R56,000 million.

The direct cost of apartheid is most clearly seen in a third measure, derived from examining state expenditures on the large, complex and active apparatus required to implement and enforce apartheid programmes. The direct annual cost of apartheid in budgeted state expenditure in the 1985/6 financial year amounted on a low estimate to R2,800 million, on a medium estimate to R3,900 million and on a high estimate to R5,700 million.

Specific areas of direct state apartheid expenditures can be identified as major contributors to its cost, but these so overlap and interlock with each other that they cannot easily be separated. At the formal apex of the apartheid state lies a complex and intricate network of legislative machinery containing the organs of direct and indirect rule. Some of the basic components of this legislative structure can be detailed to indicate its extent and complexities:

HALF THE BLACK WORKFORCE UNEMPLOYED

Academic researchers believe that there could be six million unemployed Africans – and that this is a conservative estimate. The academics criticise the government's figures for being based on the registered unemployed. As many African unemployed workers are excluded from the benefits for which people register, and as even those entitled to the benefits only receive them for six months, only a small number of unemployed Africans register as unemployed. Also, the 'independent' homelands are not included in official figures. The academics calculate that every second African worker may be jobless.

The South African political system has given birth to 13 Houses of Parliament or Legislative Assemblies, as well as the President's Council with quasi-legislative functions. There are three legislative chambers in the Central Parliament, six Legislative Assemblies in what are termed the 'non-independent black states' and four Legislative Assemblies in the 'independent states'.

Occupying seats in these 14 bodies are 1,270 members consisting of 308 members of the three Houses of the Central Parliament, 60 members of the President's Council, 501 members of the Legislative Assemblies of the 'non-independent black states' and 401 members of the Legislative Assemblies of the 'independent black states' of Transkei, Bophuthatswana, Venda and Ciskei. Of these 1,270 persons, 121 are ministers of government (approximately one in ten) and in addition there are at least 21 deputy ministers. The Central Parliament has 33 ministers, 21 cabinet ministers and 12 ministers of 'own affairs'; the 'non-independent black states' have 45 ministers and the 'independent black states' have 43 ministers.

Each of the legislative organs has government departmental structures which, by August 1986, had spawned 151 government departments in South Africa. These departments included 18 departments of health or health and welfare; 14 departments of education (under a variety of different names); 14 departments of finance or the budget; 14 departments of agriculture or agriculture and forestry; 12 departments of works and housing; 13 departments of urban affairs or local government; nine departments of economic affairs or trade and industry; five departments each of foreign affairs, transport, post and telegraphs, labour and manpower, law and order or police, defence or national security; three

87

departments of justice; one department of mineral and energy affairs; and one department of environmental affairs and tourism. Finally these 140 departments were responsible to the departments run by the 11 Presidents, Chief Ministers or Prime Ministers in South Africa. This legislative network of three Houses of Parliament and ten Legislative Assemblies, with 1,270 members, 121 ministers and 151 government departments, is not cheap to run.

Another indication of the cost of this machinery is provided by examining the rising expense of administering and running the Central Parliament. In 1981, prior to the existence of the tricameral system and the President's Council, the costs of administering Parliament and the Office of the State President, together with the salaries and allowances paid to senators and MPs, amounted to R8,720,660. By 1986, under the new constitutional system with the changed role of the State President and the President's Council and two new Houses of Parliament, the annual cost of salaries, allowances and administration had risen from R8.7 million to R40,448,000. Measured in 1980 rands this amounted to an increase of 140% over a six-year period.

Added to the costs of running the Central Parliament are those of running the legislative assemblies. As financial accounts of all of these are not easily obtained, only one comparable indication of cost can be given in the area of salaries. In the period 1984/5 the amount paid in salaries to Presidents, Vice Presidents, Chief Ministers and members of these assemblies amounted to R8,659,000. Poverty stricken areas such as QwaQwa were paying salaries of over half a million rands to members of their Legislative Assembly and other areas, such as Bophuthatswana, were paying over R1.8 million in salaries and allowances to members of their Legislative Assembly.

It is difficult to offer more than an estimate of the costs associated with the creation of 151 government departments in South Africa, particularly as one of the chief costs is in inefficiency. The fragmentation of services has produced a patchwork of badly coordinated and overlapping services and has led to the birth of additional bodies and committees in efforts to coordinate different departments' activities. This has become most evident in the area of health. It has, for instance, been reported that two hospitals, 40 km apart, were unable freely to cooperate with each other in a polio immunisation campaign during an epidemic in 1982, as they were separated by the boundary between Lebowa and Gazankulu. Cooperation required diplomatic negotiations between separate governments, while the epidemic ran its own course.

The economic cost of running 151 departments, each having separate managerial and administrative staff, separate budgets, separate accounting procedures and often providing duplicated facilities and services, is difficult to probe. The cost of duplicated services in the education sector alone were last year estimated to amount to R100 million annually by B. Dalling, MP. If one accepts this figure and applies it throughout, then the overlapping and duplicated services provided by the government departments cost South Africa over R130 million annually.

An associated and major economic cost of apartheid lies in the expenditure of the vast bureaucratic administrative apparatus involved in implementing apartheid. While all countries require a civil service to provide basic social and administrative services, the more authoritarian and regulated a society is, the greater will be its need for an army of public officials to control and administer it.

Intermeshed with the grand apartheid design of territorial segregation and the creation of so-called 'homelands' has been the policy of industrial decentralisation. This is aimed at creating jobs near or within 'homeland' boundaries so as to prevent people migrating to urban areas. Although aspects of industrial decentralisation have been intended to enforce a spread of economic development throughout South Africa, the programme forms one of the major elements of apartheid spending. It is rooted deep in apartheid ideology and is intertwined with the creation and support of ten 'homelands'. As an economic programme it has failed to produce either the jobs or the economic development required in the areas where it operates. Even the Deputy Governor of the Reserve Bank is reported to believe that industrial fragmentation, or what he termed 'decentralisation into the bush', will continue to fail as a policy.

In 1985/6 this programme cost R776.5 million to operate, R551 million of this sum being directly spent by the Department of Trade and Industry on decentralisation. In other terms, about 3 cents in every rand spent by the state is devoted to the discredited policy of Industrial Decentralisation. This again is a conservative estimate and does not take into full account the cost of the 26 government departments, development corporations and para-statals involved in running the programme, nor the large capital costs involved in its operation.

Conclusion

Many other areas of the cost of apartheid could be examined – including the enormous expense of removing over 3.5 million Africans from 'white' areas since 1960; the costs of being engaged in Namibia; the amounts spent on financing a transport system premised on geographical segregation; and the costs to individuals of having to spend long hours in travelling to work.

Yet the point is clear that the cost of apartheid, however calculated, is considerable; South Africa's resources have been squandered.

There is an immensity of tasks ahead in reconstructing this society to deal with the needs of its people. The profligate waste of resources to entrench a system of minority domination does not enable South Africa seriously to set about tackling the major problems it faces.

The critical issue is not how to lower the costs of apartheid domination and release some of the resources it consumes into the existing economic system. Rather, it is how to excise apartheid and use its squandered resources to build an equitable society. Decisions about the allocation and distribution of resources are the central political issue: who will make these decisions and who will determine the future shape of South African society? Large numbers of jobs, houses and educational opportunities can be created with the resources that South Africa is currently devoting to apartheid. The reconstruction of South African society will require a redistribution of its resources and re-ordering of its priorities.

This paper is a condensed version of Michael Savage's inaugural lecture delivered at the University of Cape Town in August 1986.

15. Conclusion

The fact that there has been a significant reduction in revolutionary violence in South Africa is proof that the State of Emergency has succeeded in curbing the revolutionary situation in South Africa, the Minister of Law and Order told Parliament in April 1989, during the budget debate of the Ministry of Law and Order.

Minister Vlok proceeded triumphantly to inform Parliament that the budget allocation of the police had gone up 28% compared with the average of 17% increase for other departments. It is safe to assume, therefore, that the level of repression in South Africa illuminated by the contributions to this booklet is not going to abate in the coming year.

Minister Vlok says that an investment of South Africa's scarce resources in the police force, during the same budget year in which Minister De Klerk announced that the attempts at the equalisation of education have been abandoned owing to the poor performance of the economy, is justified by the fact that a 'revolutionary climate' still exists in South Africa.

Vlok's statement is an admission that, in spite of the government's sophisticated repressive measures outlined above, resistance to apartheid has survived. The strategy of the government of winning the hearts and minds of the people (WHAM), which included the elimination of activists and upgrading certain townships, has hit two snags. The first one is related to sanctions against apartheid. Due to South Africa's inability to raise funds in the international capital markets (as they did when they implemented the Rive report on the upgrading of Soweto in the late 70s) and the poor performance of the economy due, inter alia, to an inability to attract international capital, the South African government has been unable to implement its upgrading programmes. The upgrading of selected townships was intended to divert the attention of the people from visible grievances and to legitimise the black local authorities by crediting the improvements in the living standards of township residents to them and their collaborationist politics.

The second snag is related to the hunger strike by detainees. This forced the government to release hundreds of detainees who otherwise would have been held until the authorities felt sure that the undemocratic and moderate leadership that was supposed to have supplanted them had taken root in the townships. The recent detainee hunger strike has, therefore, succeeded in getting a significant number of leaders of the anti-apartheid organisations out of the prisons. It has also demonstrated that action against apartheid is possible even under the most extreme conditions of repression: those of detention.

The failure of the government's repressive policies to eradicate opposition has created what one of the papers in this booklet refers to as an 'uneasy equilibrium'. One of the consequences of the strenuous opposition to apartheid in the years between 1984 and 1987 was that the government ended up by having no coherent policy except its determination to hold on to power.

At the beginning of the Botha administration the slogan was, as one of the essays points out, 'there can be no security without reform'. With the growing opposition to the government's policies this changed into 'there can be no reform without security'. Security therefore became, as all the essays show, a touchstone that informed every action of the government. Yet the South African government's repressive policies are essentially a holding operation. They are meant to create a situation – or, to use their favourite word, 'a climate' – internally and externally, that will make it possible for them to claim that they are reforming apartheid again by talking to the black 'leadership' that they have cultivated under the shield of repression. The Mass Democratic Movement in South Africa, on the retreat from state repression, is not prepared to grant the South African government the space in which it can achieve this objective. Nevertheless, one cannot be too sure about the willingness of the international community to be as steadfast on this issue as the internal opposition has been.

The South African regime's repressive 'overkill' and the indications it is giving that it cannot live without the State of Emergency are indicative of a political paralysis that has gripped it. Its retreat from the very reform that it has defined and initiated, doubtless under pressure, means that it does not have a clear vision of how South Africa can move from where it is today to achieving a reconciled and just society. This implies that the engine for change in South Africa lies outside the structures of the government and is, in fact, the mass democratic opposition that is being battered by the repressive measures outlined in this booklet. By the very

Free them all: A demonstration outside parliament in Cape Town during March 1989.

Eric Miller, Afrapix

fact of surviving South Africa's total onslaught against it, the mass democratic opposition has shown that it is the only hope for change and a better society in South Africa.

All the papers in this booklet raise the issue that, given South Africa's present repressive methods and strategies, the critical strategic intervention by the international community is to create space for the Mass Democratic Movement to continue burrowing at apartheid until it finally crumbles. Governmental policies on the South African situation must therefore be aimed at making it possible for internal opposition movements to regroup publicly and to continue the struggle to eliminate apartheid. Creating space for the opposition in South Africa clearly goes beyond the so-called positive measures that have largely characterized EEC policy at this stage. It must also involve restrictive measures designed to make it costly for the South African government to attempt to eliminate the opposition or to muzzle and shackle it as they have done since the declaration of the State of Emergency.

As for the organisations inside South Africa, the struggle continues against increasing repression. All the while, however, there is growing unity and determination to demolish the inhumane monolith of apartheid and to establish a society in South Africa where there will be human rights, democracy and an end to the rule of fear.

Postscript

T he renewal of the State of Emergency in June 1989 reaffirmed the National Party's commitment to preserving power through repressive means. In the run-up to the elections in the fourth year of the Emergency, the white leadership's squabbles led to the replacement of P.W. Botha by F.W. de Klerk. The divisions within the white community were in sharp contrast to the unity displayed by the black community around its non-violent defiance campaign against apartheid.

The defiance campaign was launched by the Mass Democratic Movement (MDM) after a successful hunger strike early in 1989 had led to the release of many detainees. The first stage of the campaign involved black patients presenting themselves for treatment at white hospitals. This was followed by blacks swimming at white beaches and using segregated transport, and black children turning up at white schools.

The MDM's defiance campaign entered a new stage a month before the 6 September general election. Restricted organisations and individuals defied their restriction orders and 'unbanned' themselves.

On the sixteenth day since the start of the defiance campaign against apartheid laws, representatives of resistance organisations set out their plans for further dramatic, coordinated protest actions... Sporting T-shirts bearing the logo of the restricted UDF (United Democratic Front), Titus Mafolo of the MDM and Ephraim Nkwe of SAYCO (South African Youth Congress) said at yesterday's press conference: "We see this as the beginning of our organisations unbanning themselves. We have chosen a peaceful, non-violent path, and will not deviate from it, even if we are met with violence."

... A group of plain-clothes policemen filmed the conference and confiscated a tape from journalist Ismail Lagardien. They said they were investigating charges of furthering the aims of a banned organisation.

In a statement the MDM called "on all organisations precluded from organising freely within their own constituencies as a result of unjust restrictions on their activities to exercise the mandate of our people to unrestrict themselves".'

Weekly Mail, 18 August 1989

The government responded predictably. They detained activists, arrested hundreds of those involved in acts of defiance and broke up peaceful meetings with teargas, rubber bullets and bird-shot.

Abbreviations

ACTWUSA	–	Amalgamated Clothing Textile Workers Union of South Africa
ANC	–	African National Congress
AZAPO	–	Azanian Peoples' Organisation
CCAWUSA	–	Commercial Catering and Allied Workers Union
CNE	–	Christian National Education
COSATU	–	Congress of South African Trade Unions
CRIC	–	Community Research and Information Centre
CWIU	–	Chemical Workers Industrial Union
DET	–	Department of Education and Training
DPSC	–	Detainees' Parents Support Committee
ECC	–	End Conscription Campaign
EEC	–	European Economic Community
FAWU	–	Food and Allied Workers Union
ICJ	–	International Commission of Jurists
IDASA	–	Institute for a Democratic Alternative for South Africa
ISA	–	Internal Security Act
JMC	–	Joint Management Council
MDM	–	Mass Democratic Movement
NACTU	–	National Council of Trade Unions
NECC	–	National Education Crisis Committee
NEHAWU	–	National Education Health and Allied Workers Union
NEUSA	–	National Education Union of South Africa
NGO	–	Non-Governmental Organisation
NIS	–	National Intelligence System
NSMS	–	National Security Management System
NUM	–	National Union of Mineworkers
NUMSA	–	National Union of Metal Workers of South Africa
POTWA	–	Post Office and Telecommunications Workers Association
PPWAWU	–	Paper, Printing, Wood and Allied Workers Union
PTSA	–	Parent/Teacher/Student Association
RSC	–	Regional Services Council
SAAWU	–	South African Allied Workers Union
SACC	–	South African Council of Churches

Abbreviations

SADF	–	South African Defence Force
SAIRR	–	South African Institution of Race Relations
SAP	–	South African Police
SARHWU	–	South African Railways and Harbours Workers Union
SCC	–	Soweto Crisis Committee
SOSCO	–	Soweto Students Congress
SRC	–	Students Representative Council
SWAPO	–	South West African People's Organisation
TGWU	–	Transport and General Workers Union
TRAC	–	Transvaal Rural Action Committee
UDF	–	United Democratic Front
UIF	–	Unemployment Insurance Fund
WHAM	–	Winning Hearts and Minds

New publications on Southern Africa from CIIR

Out of Step
War resistance in South Africa

From the age of 18, every white South African male is called up for military service: the penalty for refusing is six years' jail. OUT OF STEP tells the story of the End Conscription Campaign (ECC) and the young men who, in growing numbers, are refusing to be conscripted. As South African military power and aggresion grew in the 1970s, some young soldiers began to realise they were defending apartheid injustice. When resistance erupted in South Africa's black townships in 1984, conscripts found themselves face to face with fellow South Africans. Now it was civil war. The ECC and its young supporters brought a special brand of creative campaigning to the broad anti-apartheid struggle while walking a legal tightrope. The ranks of conscientious objectors swelled; so did popular support for the ECC. The ECC was banned in 1988; by then, war resistance had come to stay.

ECC's rapid growth and popularity are signs of hope in this crazy, crazy but beautiful country — **Archbishop Desmond Tutu**

ISBN 1 85287 053 2   price £8.99

Sanctions Against Apartheid

Who in South Africa wants sanctions? Are sanctions justified? How have sanctions come about? What do sanctions imply for the region? How do sanctions work against apartheid?

Nineteen widely published experts — from South and southern Africa, and also from Britain, Canada, the USA, and West Germany — consider the merits of sanctions from political, economic, legal, and moral points of view, at the national, regional and international levels. Their chapters:
■ trace the pro-sanctions views of unions, churches, mass political movements, and their grassroots constituents;
■ contrast the justification of sanctions and liberation efforts with South African attacks against neighbouring countries;
■ analyse the differing positions of foreign governments on sanctions, and the role of anti-apartheid campaigns abroad;
■ clarify the benefits as well as the costs of sanctions to the development and stability of the Frontline states; and
■ assess the powerful contribution of trade embargoes, restrictions on loans, and disinvestment to the forces of transformation in South Africa.
The arguments are integrated in an extensive introduction

Hardback   ISBN 1 85287 057 5   price £14.99
Paperback   ISBN 1 85287 058 3   price £7.99